ER
Extraordinary Relationships

Larry Stockstill

Bethany World Prayer Center
Baker, Louisiana
www.bethany.com

ER
by Larry Stockstill

Printed in the United States of America

ISBN 1-594679-74-6

www.xulonpress.com

I dedicate this book to the love of my life,
my wife, Melanie.
Her tireless efforts at my side while
we were missionaries in Africa
and as pastors of Bethany
have built for us a truly
"extraordinary relationship."
May every couple find the
joys of lasting relationship
that she and I are enjoying
year by year.

Contents

CHAPTER 1

Extraordinary Relationships: The Heart of the Matter Is a Matter of the Heart

Have you ever had your thoughts suddenly interrupted by the wail of an ambulance as it heads for the nearest emergency room? Have you wondered who was in trouble and how critical was the problem? Maybe you even bowed your head for a minute and breathed a silent prayer for the nameless victim of the unknown emergency. You probably never found out what happened in that particular situation, but you knew when you heard the siren that a state of emergency existed.

A state of emergency exists within the institution of the family! Weekly in the news, the alarm sounds of increasing divorce rates, abandoned children, and poverty in the midst of the most affluent society on earth. Something has gone terribly wrong. And as unbelievable as it may seem, the Christian family fares no better. Unless something changes, a crisis of unimaginable proportions looms ahead.

Just as the person who faces a medical emergency must receive immediate intervention if he is to survive, so, too, must we act now to stop this downward spiral of the family. The actions taken to preserve a life are swift, decisive, and drastic, and the measures we must take to save our families can be no less.

That is my goal in writing this small book: that you would learn simple, effective tools that you can implement *now* in your family. Your family doesn't have to spend its time in the "emergency room" of life, going from one crisis to another, forever trying to apply Band-Aids to the gaping wounds of the heart. No, there's a better way. I trust that as you read this book, your family will move from the "ER" of crisis to the "ER" of *extraordinary relationships* in Christ.

The Condition of the Heart

Any discussion of the family has got to start with the condition of the heart, or core, of the family. In the physical body, the heart is perhaps the most important organ. Traditionally, we determine life or death based on the function of this organ. Four main arteries serve the heart, and as long as they are free of blockage and blood can flow unhindered through them, the heart usually works just fine. But if those arteries are blocked by excessive cholesterol or become narrow and constricted with age, the health and capacity of the heart are severely impaired. If the blockage becomes too great, the person may suffer a heart attack and even require bypass surgery to compensate for the blockage within the arteries. The health of the heart is vital to the health of the entire body.

In a similar fashion, if the very heart of your family relationships is healthy, then your family is healthy. On the other hand, if there is something wrong within your heart or the heart of a family member, then the relationships within your family are going to be strained. It's actually quite simple: The condition of the heart is the crux of healthy family relationships. In other words, the heart of the matter is really a matter of the heart! If you will examine your heart and remove blockages that are hampering you, you will experience a free flow of the Holy Spirit in your life, and your family relationships will truly become extraordinary relationships!

The Hardening of the Heart

In Matthew 19:8 NKJV, Jesus addressed the issue of hardness of heart and how it affects families. After reiterating God's original plan of one man and one woman joined together as one flesh, Jesus answered the Pharisees' question concerning why Moses had allowed divorce. Jesus said, "Moses, because of the hardness of your hearts, permitted you to divorce your wives, but from the beginning it was not so." Divorce with its resultant shattering of families was never God's intent, but it was allowed only because of the condition of hardness of heart.

Just as improper diet, lack of exercise, or genetic predisposition can cause the arteries of your physical heart to become hard and brittle and lose their elasticity, certain things can happen in your spirit that cause you to become hard and bitter. Let's look at what, I believe, are the four most important factors that cause your heart to become hard and callous.

Selfishness Instead of Serving

The first thing that can harden your heart is selfishness. Although selfishness may seem like a self-explanatory word, it bears looking into a little bit more. Selfishness is really the opposite of serving. Jesus addressed this issue with two of His disciples in Matthew 20. James and John, along with their mother, approached Jesus, jockeying for positions of honor in His kingdom. The Lord gently rebuked them, saying, "Whoever desires to become great among you, let him be your servant. And whoever desires to be first among you, let him be your slave—just as the Son of Man did not come to be served, but to serve, and to give His life a ransom for many" (vv. 27–28 NKJV).

Jesus' entire ministry was wrapped up in that one word: serving. It characterized who He was and what He stood for. If your heart is a heart of service and your desire is to help others any way you can, then your heart will remain tender and soft. If, on the other hand, your heart is characterized by selfishness and self-centeredness, then you will become hardhearted and inflexible, thinking only of yourself. *My* time, *my* agenda, *my* money, *my* career—all these phrases are the benchmark of a person whose heart is basically selfish.

Too many people make all their decisions based solely on themselves and what they want to do. Everyone else in their families or on their jobs is secondary to them; they just expect everybody to adapt to the decisions they make. But when you are in relationship with people, your decisions not only affect you, but they also affect everyone around you. You cannot make decisions independent of their impact on others.

Jesus taught us the beauty of serving others when He so humbly washed His disciples' feet in John 13. The one who had come from the right hand of the Father and deserved the praise and adoration of the world knelt before these men of flesh and washed their dirty feet. What an example of unselfish, unpretentious service!

In our families, there is no place for power struggles, with husbands trying to lord it over their wives and wives trying to manipulate their husbands. Instead, we should have husbands, wives, and even children all trying to outdo one another in giving and serving. When that dynamic is operating in a family, the entire atmosphere changes.

Can you imagine what *your* family would be like if you woke up tomorrow morning and everyone in your family was totally concentrated on serving the other family members? What if your spouse asked you, "What are your plans for today? Can I help you with them?" What if your children asked, "Do you need me to do anything, Mom and Dad? Would you like something to drink? I'll get it for you." I know some of you would think you had awakened in the wrong bed if that happened, but it would be pretty amazing, wouldn't it?

Most of you probably remember the movie called *How the Grinch Stole Christmas.* Based on the children's book of the same title written by Dr. Seuss, the movie features a mean, old grinch with a tiny, hard heart. In the course of the movie, however, a series of events causes the Grinch's heart to grow bigger and bigger until by the end of the movie, the Grinch has been totally transformed. His teeny little heart changes into a great big heart overflowing with love and concern for others. What an apt picture of the power of love and serving to remove the blockage of selfishness from any hard heart!

Rejection Instead of Respecting

The second blockage that can exist in your heart is rejection. Rejection, basically, is the feeling you get when someone doesn't respect you. Rejection can happen when you're a child, or it can occur when you're eighty years old. You can be rejected on your job, or you can be rejected at home. Regardless of the source of rejection, you lose your sense of self-worth and acceptance when you are not treated with honor, dignity, or respect.

An interesting thing I've noticed about rejection is that rejection demands further rejection. People who are suffering from rejection often set themselves up for more of it. Because there is something wounded in their hearts, they do not see themselves as worthy individuals. So wherever they go, they expect that others will reject them. They're looking for it around every corner. Without even realizing it, they begin acting in ways that cause people to not want to be around them. They build walls around themselves in an effort to protect themselves, but really, all those walls do is keep others out.

Rejected people are often angry, aloof, and uncooperative. Their inner hurt leads them to draw back from developing real relationships with others, even in their families. In fact, rejection sustained within the family is probably the deepest rejection of all, especially when that rejection comes from a parent. The father, in particular, plays a pivotal role in affirming his children and building their self-image. If affirmation from the father is lacking, the child's concept of himself as a worthwhile individual is greatly hindered.

I've known a particular NFL football player for years. He's a big man—6 feet 7 inches tall and 280 pounds of solid rock. When he speaks, he has this big, booming voice that just seems to resonate from some place deep within him. He causes quite a stir wherever he goes, merely because of his impressive physical size. This man is a wonderful man, secure in who he is in Jesus, but he has a testimony that many are not aware of. This big old guy—so tough and masculine-looking—walked around for years with a hurt inside of him from something that his father had done.

From the time that this man began playing football, his father never attended one of his games. All through elementary school, high school, college, and then even in the pros, this man was hurt because his father never came to watch him play. Finally one day his dad called him and said, "I'm coming to your game." He was so excited to have his father finally come to a game. Knowing his dad was in the stands watching him, he said, made him play like a wild man that day. During the game, he blocked a field goal, sacked the quarterback, and got five unassisted tackles. He played his heart out, hoping his father would be proud of him. After the game, the young man ran to his father in the stands, eagerly anticipating the affirmation he had longed for all his life. His dad, however, did not reach out to hug him, nor did he give him a congratulatory slap on the back. His father simply stood there looking at him, then said, "Son, you could have played a lot better than you did today."

Perhaps his father thought he would spoil his son with complimentary words, or maybe he mistakenly thought he was urging his son to higher achievement, but when he spoke those critical words to his boy, something died in that young man's heart. The rejection was so painful that from that time on, the young man's life spiraled downward. Eventually, he did get saved and God healed the wound, but the rejection, nevertheless, was devastating.

Rejection and its awful consequences are also found in the Bible. In the familiar Old Testament story of Jacob and Esau, we see sibling rivalry at its worst in the lives of these twin boys. Jacob was born second, and all through his growing-up years, he struggled with his desire to be No. 1. His brother, Esau, was favored by their father, Isaac. As the oldest, Esau possessed the birthright, but Jacob wanted it. Because of the feeling of being second best, Jacob went through life manipulating and deceiving to get what he wanted. Not until he had a face-to-face encounter with God was Jacob able to overcome the rejection that had dominated his life.

That's how it is with you, too. If you have a wound of rejection in your heart (and most of us do in one area or another), then you will subconsciously behave in such a way that causes people to reject you. When they do you wrong, you think, "I knew that was coming." Then you withdraw and don't want to open up to anybody anymore. You don't want to give too much of yourself for fear of being hurt, and your heart grows smaller and smaller and harder and harder.

There is one, however, who knows your pain. Jesus understands like no one else the anguish you carry deep in your heart. When He hung on the cross, not only did He suffer abandonment from most of His earthly companions, but He also experienced the ultimate rejection when the Father had to turn His back for the moment when Jesus bore the sins of the world. Jesus' heartrending cry to the Father, "My God, My God, why have You forsaken Me?" (Matt. 27:46 NKJV), is the very epitome of the agony of rejection. No matter what you have suffered, it cannot equal the magnitude of Jesus' rejection. But unless you allow the Lord to heal you of rejection, you will always be controlled by it.

Bitterness Instead of Blessing

A third blockage in the heart that can ruin relationships is bitterness. As a pastor, I've seen the results of bitterness in a person's heart many, many times. Bitterness is really a lot like heartburn. When you hold a grudge against someone, you cannot even bear the mention of that person's name. Just to hear the name of the one who hurt you causes an upsurge of burning anger to rise within you. It spontaneously comes alive on the inside, and you are enflamed with ill feelings and unforgiveness. That bitterness eats away at you, always there like a nagging case of indigestion.

If you make a decision not to forgive someone, your life stops at that point. You don't move any further than that. If you choose to hold bitterness inside, you're like a train that has jumped the track. You are off course and sidelined until you release the hurt and get back on track with your life.

That's exactly where many of you are today. Someone hurt you deeply, and you have never been able to let go of it. Maybe a relative molested you when you were a child, or maybe your spouse has verbally or physically abused you. Maybe you were denied a rightful inheritance, or maybe your spouse was unfaithful to you. The list could go on and on because there are literally thousands of ways people hurt one another. But the only way you will move past the heartaches and injustices of life is to make a conscious decision to release and forgive when someone hurts you.

Forgiveness is a choice, not an emotion. If you are bound and determined to hold a debt of unforgiveness against someone, that relationship becomes a curse in your life. It truly harms you much more than it does the one you are angry with. Some of you have been sitting on the sidelines of life for years, and the bitterness in your heart is just as great as it was the day you were hurt. Life has lost its vibrancy, and you simply plod along, one day pretty much like the next. It's like your heart is shrinking, unable to love others or enjoy life.

If that describes you, I challenge you to recall Jesus' words as He was dying on the cross: "Father, forgive them, for they know not what they do." There hung Jesus—totally exposed and vulnerable. Despite the agony of His physical torment, the ridicule heaped upon Him, and the mocking directed against Him, He uttered those unforgettable words: "Father, forgive them." I would never want to make light of your pain; nevertheless, whatever you have been through is not nearly as horrible as what Christ endured on your behalf. He set the standard for forgiveness when He did the unthinkable and released those who had crucified Him.

Some of you are probably saying right about now, "Well, you can't just go around forgiving everybody for everything." To that I dare answer, "Oh, yes you can!" In fact, you have to do just that if you want to keep progressing in your life. Time stops for those who refuse to forgive. But even after you forgive, you've actually got to go a step further and start speaking blessings over those who have hurt you. To bless them means to pray for them and to hold no record of wrongs against them. That might take you some time, but if you first make a conscious decision in your heart to forgive them, eventually you will be able to not only forgive, but also to bless. When you do that, the last remains of bitterness in your heart will crumble.

Lust Instead of Loyalty

The last blockage that can make your heart hard is lust. Lust will effectively shut down your heart. When you allow lust to dwell inside you, it constricts your ability to be tender and to truly love. Lust destroys relationships because it destroys trust.

Relationships of real love are characterized by commitment, loyalty, and faithfulness. In the context of marriage, such relationships include a pure, pleasurable sex life, as God intended. But if partners in a marriage yield to lustful thoughts or actions, they become concerned only with gratifying themselves. Their hearts are no longer concerned with their partners, but only with getting their physical desires met. Lust in a relationship makes the person engaging in it more like an animal than a human, controlled by base desire rather than loving commitment.

The stories of those who have been destroyed by lust are too numerous to record. You probably know many people who have shipwrecked their homes, marriages, and relationships because of uncontrolled lust in their hearts. That's where lust originates: the heart. Jesus said so in Mark 7:21–23: "For from within, out of the heart of men, proceed evil thoughts, adulteries, fornications, murders, thefts, covetousness, wickedness, deceit, lasciviousness, an evil eye, blasphemy, pride, foolishness: All these evil things come from within, and defile the man." Before lust is ever acted upon in the form of fornication or adultery, it has first been entertained in the heart. That is why we are admonished by the Scriptures, "Keep thy heart with all diligence; for out of it are the issues of life" (Prov. 4:23).

David, in the Bible, is a prime example of the destructiveness of lust in relationships. In 2 Samuel 11, the entire sordid affair is recorded. King David had everything he could possibly want in life. He possessed money, position, influence, and friends. But one day he saw a woman, Bathsheba, taking a bath, and he wanted her for himself, even though she was the wife of his friend Uriah. He sent for her, and David and Bathsheba committed adultery, never realizing that she would become pregnant with David's child. When David learned of the pregnancy, he contrived circumstances to have Uriah killed in battle in an attempt to cover his sin. That shows you how hard and unfeeling the heart can become as a result of lust. David didn't care about his friend anymore. He was even willing to have him murdered so that he could take Uriah's wife as his own.

Loyalty, rather than lust, however, is the basis for God-honoring relationships. Jesus remained loyal to His friends even though they betrayed Him. He demonstrated His loyalty to His mother by making provision for her care as He hung dying on the cross. And He forgave those who put Him to death, remaining true to the will of His Father.

Lust, bitterness, rejection, and selfishness—that's the diagnosis concerning a hardened heart. Any one of these four things can block your heart and keep the love and grace of God from flowing in your relationships. But the good news is that God wants to remove those blockages. He wants your heart to be soft again so that you can love and have extraordinary relationships in your family. He wants you to be free, and He wants to heal your heart. He wants to change you from the inside out, and in His gracious kindness, He has provided the perfect plan.

A Heart of Flesh Instead of a Heart of Stone

There are three things that will soften your heart and make it tender, and you can find these in Ezekiel 36:25–27.

Cleansing (v. 25)

In verse 25, the Word of God says, "Then will I sprinkle clean water upon you, and ye shall be clean: from all your filthiness, and from all your idols, will I cleanse you." Notice the first word in that verse: then. That implies that something happened before, but now God is going to do something different. God is the only one who can cleanse the past. All of us have done so many things to damage relationships, but God says He will cleanse us. That cleansing comes from the blood of Christ. Hebrews 10:22 says that by the precious blood of Jesus, our hearts are sprinkled, or cleansed, from an evil conscience. That means that *everything* in your past can be cleansed by the blood of Jesus. Everything! What an awesome thought!

Changing (v. 26)

After God cleanses you, He does something just as remarkable: He changes you! Verse 26 says, "A new heart also will I give you, and a new spirit will I put within you: and I will take away the stony heart out of your flesh, and I will give you an heart of flesh." That goes beyond what you could ever imagine. Not only will God forgive you and cleanse your heart, but He will also actually perform a heart transplant within you! You will be changed on the inside so that those blockages within your heart no longer exist.

When you submit your heart to God, it's like He says, "Hey, just give me that old heart of yours. I've cleaned it up; now just give me that old rejection, that old bitterness, that old selfishness, that old lust that's been controlling you. Just let me take that thing and get rid of it for you, and I'll put a brand-new heart on the inside of you." That's really what being born again means. It means a change so great on the inside that it's like you are getting to start all over in life. You're the same person on the outside, but God so changes you on the inside, that it's as though you are being born anew, starting from scratch with a clean slate. That's what God calls giving you a heart of flesh.

Filling (v. 27)

Now we come to the best part of the passage from Ezekiel. Verse 27 says, "I will put my spirit within you, and cause you to walk in my statutes, and ye shall keep my judgments, and do them." The Lord says, "Yes, I'm going to wash away your past, and yes, I'm going to give you a brand-new heart. But I'm going to do something even greater. I'm going to put my Holy Spirit within you, and He is going to write My law on your heart." In other words, when God fills you with the Holy Spirit, He changes your "want to." You look the same on the outside, but when the Holy Spirit dwells on the inside, you don't want to do the same things anymore. Instead of wanting to be selfish, you want to give. Instead of being angry and bitter, you want to forgive.

The changes in relationships would be phenomenal if we would allow the Holy Spirit to fill us with His presence. I can just imagine a man who gets full of the Holy Spirit who suddenly wants to serve his wife. I can see him bringing her breakfast in bed, and I can just imagine her total amazement at the change in her husband. I can envision wives, too, wanting to serve their husbands when they come home tired from a hard day at work. I can even see children going to their parents and asking if they can do anything to help around the house. I can see the Holy Spirit bringing families together, and family members trying to outdo one another in serving. I can see families receiving and respecting one another and being loyal and committed to one another. I can see everything changing in a family because the Holy Spirit is in control.

Within your own power, you can change nothing, but when the Holy Spirit takes up residence within you, He can change everything. He births within you both the desire and ability to change, and it becomes natural for you to serve, to respect, to bless, and to commit. He is the one who can change your hard, stony heart into a heart of flesh, and He is the one who can give you extraordinary relationships!

CHAPTER 2

Extraordinary Emotions: The Key to Healthy Relationships

Healthy relationships start in the heart. Once your heart is healed, however, you can move on to specific areas of your life that affect the quality of your relationships. I have discovered that the third chapter of Ecclesiastes has a lot to say that is quite relevant to relationships. The timeless words of this well-known passage begin with the words "To everything there is a season, and a time to every purpose under the heaven." The middle of verse three continues with the thought that there is "a time to break down, and a time to build up."

In developing extraordinary relationships, first you break down those things that are causing your heart to become hard. You get rid of selfishness, rejection, bitterness, and lust. Then after that, God builds you up by cleansing you, creating a new heart within you, and filling you with His Spirit. All this takes place in your heart, or what we call your spirit. It is the place where you begin.

On the heels of getting your heart healed, however, God begins working to restore your emotions. Emotions reside in your soul—not your spirit—and your soul is composed of three parts: mind, will, and emotions. When your emotions are healthy, then your relationships flourish; when your emotions are distorted or out of control, then your relationships suffer.

Emotions are a very important part of who you are. God created you to have emotions because He has them, too. Now I know that's a new thought to some of you, but God really does have emotions. When God saw the wickedness of mankind as recorded in Genesis 6:6, "it grieved him at his heart." The NIV says, "His heart was filled with pain," and the NLT says, "It broke his heart." He obviously felt great sorrow over the condition of the world.

We also see deep emotion in the life of Jesus. In Matthew 23:37, you can just hear the grief in His voice in His poignant words spoken over Jerusalem: "O Jerusalem, Jerusalem . . . how often would I have gathered thy children together, even as a hen gathereth her chickens under her wings, and ye would not!" At the tomb of Lazarus, Jesus wept, and those present commented on His love for His friend (John 11:35–36). His agony of heart and deep distress in the Garden of Gethsemane are clearly evident in the Gospels of Matthew, Mark, and Luke. Jesus was a man of intense emotion, and He was not afraid to express it.

Emotions reflect the health and depth of a relationship. When the woman in Simon's house washed Jesus' feet with her tears, her emotions revealed the intensity of her relationship with Jesus (Luke 7). Because she had been forgiven much, her love and gratitude to Jesus simply overflowed. The depth of her love was revealed through her emotions, or in other words, her emotions were a mirror into her soul.

If you want to have extraordinary relationships—not just average, surface-type relationships—then you are going to have to learn how to discern emotions and how to use them in a constructive manner. When you are sensitive to a person's emotions, your relationship begins to grow and deepen. It begins moving from a "Hi, how are you?" type of relationship to a "What can I do to help you?" kind of relationship. But it is going to take a commitment on your part to see this happen.

The word *relationship* is derived from the root word *relate.* If you can't relate well to your mate, your children, or your extended family, then you will never have meaningful relationships with them. People tell me all the time, "Well, our family is just kind of like ships in a harbor. We pass by one another every now and then but have very little contact. We sleep in the same house, and we bump into one another in the kitchen a couple of times a day, but that's about it." That, my brothers and sisters, is not relationship!

Emotions provide guideposts and signals within a relationship. Until you can recognize the emotions of your partner, you will never attain intimacy in your marriage. Emotions are good and even necessary in relationships, and therein lies the problem for some of you. You're afraid of emotions. You'd rather have people "behave" and keep their emotions to themselves. Maybe you were trained that way as a child. Statements like "Big boys don't cry" and "Crying is a sign of weakness" cause many people, especially men, to grow up with a distorted view of emotions.

A Time to Weep and a Time to Laugh

But look at what the Bible says about emotions in Romans 12:15: "Rejoice with them that do rejoice, and weep with them that weep." Or back in our third chapter of Ecclesiastes, verse 4 says that there is "a time to weep, and a time to laugh; a time to mourn, and a time to dance." Emotions are not only tolerated but also validated in the Word of God! So you are going to have to learn how to read the signals that your family members give you through their emotions if you want to have meaningful relationships with them.

It's those flashes of emotion, good or bad, that provide insight on how to deepen your relationships. If you miss a signal or respond to it incorrectly, you can damage the relationship. You have to learn to be sensitive enough to observe the emotion and then to respond to it correctly. Proverbs 25:20 NKJV says this about someone who responds inappropriately to an emotion: "Like one who takes away a garment in cold weather, and like vinegar on soda, is one who sings songs to a heavy heart." In other words, there's a time and a season for everything, and you must be timely in the way you respond to the emotional state of people. If you miss it and are out of season with your response, you only hurt them. It's like rubbing salt in a wound.

Unfortunately, I see this pattern of response all too often in too many relationships. People are awkward in the way they discern what's going on around them. They have no clue as to the "season" and thus respond in a totally unsatisfactory manner. It's like wearing shorts in the dead of winter: that's a totally inappropriate way of dressing for the season. If you don't dress in sync with the weather, you're going to be very uncomfortable, at the least, and you might even cause harm to your body by your inappropriate dress. In the same way, you've got to be able to discern the emotional state of your loved ones; otherwise, you can cause great damage in your family relationships.

The book of Job gives a vivid illustration of poor relating in a relationship. In the beginning of his awful trial, Job had the support of his friends. They were in the right time and right season in relating to him. Look at what Job 2:12–13 says: "And when they lifted up their eyes afar off, and knew him not, they lifted up their voice, and wept; and they rent every one his mantle, and sprinkled dust upon their heads toward heaven. So they sat down with him upon the ground seven days and seven nights, and none spake a word unto him: for they saw that his grief was very great." That's pretty impressive! Job's friends knew that he had lost all his money, his children, and even his health. They knew that the last thing Job needed was somebody lecturing him on what he had done wrong to bring such tragedy upon himself.

Unfortunately, his friends were unable to sustain their unconditional support of Job, and later in the book, they offered many reasons and explanations as to why Job was in such a tragic circumstance. Even Job's wife failed him in his time of trial, saying in verse 9 of the second chapter, "Dost thou still retain thine integrity? Curse God, and die." How's that for a totally off-the-wall response? No support, no encouragement, no empathy—just "Curse God and die"!

In your marriage, the last thing your spouse needs is for you to try to be the Holy Spirit. You don't need to be constantly criticizing your spouse, telling him all the little helpful tips you have as to how he could better himself. You don't need to tell him all his flaws and what he should be doing to correct them. No, you don't need to do that at all. Leave that to the Holy Spirit, and you find a way to relate to your spouse in an affirming manner. Build him up; don't tear him down. When he is going through a rough spot, walk through it with him. You don't have to have all the answers, and you might not even need to say a word—just be there for him. Know when to weep with him, and know when to laugh with him. Discern the emotion and respond in a loving way. And, of course, all that applies to both husbands and wives.

Passion: Pain and Pleasure

Our verse from Ecclesiastes 3:4 tells us that there is "a time to weep, and a time to laugh." These are the two basic passions that people express. There are things that cause us great pain, and there are other things that bring us great pleasure. We are constantly moving between these two emotions, and sometimes the transition is quite rapid. Have you ever observed people at a football game when their team is losing by six points? They are sitting there, so sad, frustrated, and upset because their team is behind. They are people in pain! Then suddenly their team makes an interception and runs the ball all the way back for a touchdown. The pain flies out the window, and the joy is uncontainable. In that brief span of time, those people went from the depths of despair to the heights of elation.

Because people can fluctuate so quickly and wildly between these two extremes of emotion, we have to become students of their behavior. When we recognize what they are experiencing, a sense of closeness and intimacy develops. When we fail to discern the emotion, however, a distance creeps into the relationship. The bottom line is that we have to be able to recognize others' pain and pleasure and respond appropriately.

When you go to the doctor because of pain in your body, he does a thorough examination to locate the source of the pain. First he pushes in one place, and then he prods in another. Then all of a sudden, he pushes in one particular spot and you practically jump off the examination table. The doctor has found the source of your pain! It may not be visible to the naked eye, but the doctor knows that there is something wrong beneath the surface that caused you to react so dramatically. If he can correctly diagnose the cause of your pain, then he can suggest a remedy to alleviate it.

That's just the way you have to be in your relationships. You have to be able to recognize and know how to deal with the sources of others' pain. You're going to have to know what questions to ask and where to prod to be able to diagnose and relieve their pain.

Three Sources of Private Pain

I have found that there are three main responses that signal when someone is in pain. If you will learn to recognize these reactions and use them to correctly diagnose the real problem, you can start building truly extraordinary relationships.

Anger

The first response you might notice in someone who is in pain is anger. Angry people are hurting people, and they need to have their anger acknowledged. Don't you just hate it when something upsets you and makes you angry, but no one in your family notices or seems to care? It makes you even angrier that your feelings are being ignored, and if you're like most people, you kick the anger reaction up a notch or two. You are bound and determined that everyone is going to know that you are angry. It's kind of like that old saying "If Mama ain't happy, then nobody's happy." You want that feeling acknowledged.

Frustration is at the root of most anger. When a person has an angry outburst, he's really saying, "I'm frustrated, but nobody's noticing." He has goals that he is unable to reach because people seemingly keep blocking his progress. Because of this inability to accomplish the goal, the person becomes angry.

An all too common scenario illustrating this link between frustration and anger is often played out in a home on Sunday morning when the family is getting ready for church. The husband has a goal to leave the house by a certain time in order to get to church on time. He gets himself ready, and then he begins waiting on his wife to get ready. Thirty minutes before time to leave, he's pacing in the living room. Twenty minutes left, and he walks into the bedroom, looking for his wife. Ten minutes before departure time, and he just can't stand it anymore. He bursts into the bathroom and shouts at his wife, "What's taking so long? Let's go, let's go, let's go! We're going to be late!" He is a man in pain, and boy, is he frustrated!

Women, of course, get frustrated, too, and, like men, may react in anger. We see this in the familiar Scripture story of Mary and Martha. These two women, along with their brother Lazarus, were close friends of Jesus. Martha was a hard worker, and when Jesus visited their home, she wanted everything to be just right for Him. Her agenda included a clean house, a big meal, and a hospitable atmosphere. Her plan included her sister's help to accomplish all these tasks.

Mary, however, did not have the same outlook as Martha and chose to sit at Jesus' feet, listening to His words. Martha, busy with all the serving, became distraught that her sister was not helping her with the work and complained to Jesus about it. She was so frustrated that her goals were not being accomplished that she missed the chance to deepen her relationship with the Savior!

If you are living with someone who seems to be angry all the time, it is so important that you ask the Lord to show you the cause of the person's anger. The anger is only an outward indication of an inward frustration. Find out the source of the anger and you'll identify the real frustration. Then you can ask the Lord to show you how to heal that hurt and how to deepen your level of intimacy with the person.

Depression

A second thing that alerts you to the fact that someone is in pain is depression. Depression, however, is not always obvious. The person might not speak about his pain, but might just keep it bottled inside. If you notice a lack of motivation in someone in your family, many times that is a clue that he is depressed. The depressed person has lost hope and thus motivation for change; that is the real reason for his depression. He is usually his own worst critic, keeping an account of every way in which he has failed. He doesn't feel like he can accomplish anything of real value, so he just stops trying after a while. The depressed person lives with regrets over past failures.

A person in the pain of depression cannot see the good in life or in anything he has accomplished. If you try to compliment him on a job well-done, he counters with, "Aw, I could have done better." If you try to encourage him for a brighter future, he sighs, "No, nothing's going to change. I've made too many mistakes and messed up too many times." He is negative and pessimistic because he is in the grip of a private pain.

If someone in your family is depressed, you might notice that he doesn't want to get out of the bed in the morning. He loses interest in things that formerly brought him much enjoyment. To him, life has become drudgery, and everything seems hopeless and futile. When a family member is feeling like this, you can't just go up to him and say, "What's the matter with you? Snap out of it!" You can't just offer useless advice like "Don't be depressed." You can't just go singing merrily around the house, ignoring the other person's pain.

What you actually need to do is first acknowledge that person's pain. Go up to him and say, "I can see you're a little down today. Would you like to talk about it?" Listen to him and empathize with him. You don't have to have the answer to his problem, but if you let him know that you are there for him, the relationship will begin to grow in intimacy. The person is validated because you recognized his pain and made a genuine effort to share it.

Fear

The third factor that signals emotional pain is fear. Fear usually has its roots in a trauma that a person suffered in which there was no one to protect him. The traumatic event often lies buried deep inside and is manifested outwardly in irrational fears. If you're living with someone who is full of fear, you can't just look at him like he's crazy and say, "What's your problem? Get a grip!" No, you've got to back up, slow down, and find out why the person is so afraid.

The fear probably began when the individual endured a horrible event but had no one to protect him. He was forced to go through it alone, and as a result, he erected defenses in his heart. He made up his mind that he would never again allow himself to be in a position where he could be hurt. Subsequently, he tries to handle his problems without help from anyone else, but he is unable to do so, and fear soon becomes a generalized fact of life for him. His unresolved fear destroys much of the joy in life, and it prevents real intimacy from ever materializing in his relationships.

It doesn't matter whether the problem is anger, depression, or fear. What people are looking for is someone who will notice their pain and take the time to try to help. So when you notice that someone in your family is hurting, you can't just act like the problem doesn't exist and hope that it will go away. It's cruel to ignore it or to run roughshod over the person, demanding him to shape up and get with the program.

If you want extraordinary family relationships, then you've got to become a student of your family's ways. You've got to always be looking for the signals they're sending that tell you when they have a need. And when you see the signal, you've got to enter into their pain and share it with them. There is a "time to weep," and once you understand that, you are well on your way to building intimate, loving extraordinary relationships.

Three Sources of Private Pleasure

There is, indeed, "a time to weep" with someone, but

there is just as surely "a time to laugh." In fact, it is the complementary thought with a "time to weep" in Ecclesiastes 3:4. Life is full of weeping and laughing, joy and sorrow, mourning and dancing. It is the very nature of life to go through both good times and bad. But when you have extraordinary family relationships, you always have someone with whom to share both kinds of situations.

If you pay careful attention and observe your family members, you can learn what makes them happy and then you can participate in it, just like you do with their sorrows. The bond that is created in this way is different, but no less important, than the bond that is created by helping carry someone's burden. Although the particulars will differ from person to person, I have discovered that there are three main sources of pleasure.

Hobbies

Hobbies reflect a person's interests. When a person is genuinely interested in something, he doesn't mind devoting time to it. To him, it's a pleasure and a joy to engage in that particular activity. Nobody has to force him to do it; he just wants to. Whenever that subject that he's interested in comes up, he gets all excited. He starts jumping into the conversation and loves to talk all about that thing that so captivates him.

In a family, not everyone is interested in the same thing. Different things appeal to different people, and that's the way it should be. But if you want outstanding relationships in your family, you are going to have to learn what your spouse and children really love doing and then participate in those hobbies with them.

That's what I'm trying to do in my family. Two of my sons, for instance, love golf. It just so happens that golf is not really one of my favorite pastimes. But at Christmas one year, the staff at church gave me a set of golf clubs, and as I looked at those clubs, the first thing that came to mind was how much my two oldest sons love golf. So I thought, "Well, I might as well give it a try. What do I have to lose, as long as there aren't too many houses near the golf course?"

So we went out together to play golf. Now it wasn't that I really wanted to play golf, but I wanted to be with my sons, doing what interested them. I wanted to share their enjoyment of the game, so I went. Up to this point, my technique in golf had always been to just "grip it and rip it"! Some of you know what I mean. I was just happy to hit the ball any way I could. That was my sole objective.

But on this day when I went with my sons, a true miracle happened on the thirteenth hole! I was busy concentrating on everything my boys were telling me to do, so I didn't notice at first where the ball went after I took my shot. I was just happy I hit it. But when I looked up, there was the ball, right next to the green. I walked over to it for my next play, and the boys said, "Dad, you need to chip the next shot." I didn't know what that meant, but they handed me a club, I hit the ball, and it rolled to within four feet of the hole. So now I was putting for par! All was quiet on the green. My sons handed me my new putter. I gripped it just right, I tapped the ball, and nothing but the bottom of the cup! My first par!

I was not prepared for what happened next. My grown sons began to whoop and holler and carry on right there on the green! They were so excited and their enthusiasm was so contagious that before I knew it, I was joining in with them. There we were—high-fiving each other and jumping around like rabbits! Daddy's first par! If I had known the kind of joy that such a simple thing would bring my sons, I would have started playing golf with them a long time ago. I had entered into their pleasure, and as a result, we all benefited.

When you discover what makes someone in your family happy and you participate in it, you deepen the relationship significantly. But if you do your thing and your spouse and children do their things, then you miss out on the joy of sharing in something that is meaningful to them. You can have ordinary relationships that way, but you'll never have extraordinary relationships unless you participate in one another's interests.

Another example from my family of the benefits of sharing someone's pleasure concerns my wife, Melanie. Melanie loves poetry, and several years ago I began noticing that she kept ordering poetry books. She could sit and read the stuff for hours, whereas the thought of all those poems and flowery words put me to sleep! One day we were sitting in our home, and Melanie was reading her poetry book. All of a sudden, she looked over at me and said, "Would you like me to read some poetry to you?" Now my natural, self-centered inclination was to say, "That's quite all right, Sweetheart. You don't need to do that, but thank you anyway." But when Melanie asked me that question, I discerned that reading poetry gave her great pleasure and she wanted to share that with me. So I said, "Sure, read me some poetry. I'd love to hear it." I sat there and listened to her read a poem, seeing what great joy it gave her to share with me something that was important to her. And I've been listening to her read poetry ever since!

Her interest in poetry grew into a desire to visit the places where her favorite poets had lived and written their poems. So for our twenty-fifth wedding anniversary, we visited England, the home of Lord Tennyson, William Wordsworth, and so many other great poets. We rented a car and I drove on the left side of the road, just to get Melanie to the Lake District where her beloved poets had lived. I went through Wordsworth's house with her, learning all about him and sharing the experience with Melanie.

When we went to Lord Tennyson's home, something happened that was so sweet that I'll never forget it. We arrived at the place, and there was this little brook next to the house. To me, it was just a small, nondescript ditch with water running through it, but to Melanie, it was something entirely different. Gazing at that little stream of water, she began exclaiming excitedly, "The brook, the brook! Oh, look! It's the brook!" Then she was overcome with emotion and began to cry. "That's the brook!" she whispered, awe-struck, and then she proceeded to quote from her favorite Tennyson poem, entitled "The Brook." Melanie was so overjoyed with the sheer pleasure of the moment that she just reached over, grabbed me, and hugged me really hard. I had entered her world and shared what was for her a very special, indescribable moment.

If I had never been willing to listen to her read poetry and if I had never made the effort to try to understand why she loved it so much, I would have missed that unforgettable moment. But because we shared it together, our relationship deepened and grew richer. I saw the world through her eyes and understood a little better something that was important to her. Her joy was so tangible that it made me want to explore her love for books and literature all the more.

Men, that's what you've got to do in your family. Find out what your wife truly enjoys and then participate in it with her. If she loves to shop (thank God, Melanie doesn't!), then go to the mall with her, look at all the stuff she "oohs" and "ahs" over, hold her hand as you walk around, and take pleasure in seeing her enjoy herself.

Ladies, the same holds true for you. If your husband loves football, for example, don't just say, "Oh, I don't care about all that sports stuff." Don't dismiss what is important to him. Take the time to learn the basic rules of the game, and watch a game or two with him. Don't miss the opportunity to be a part of something that he enjoys.

One of the reasons that people get divorced is that they fail to share in their spouses' pain or pleasure. They fail to relate at the times when their spouses' emotions are soft and vulnerable. They ignore their pain or dismiss their pleasure.

It's like a door. You can either open the door into your spouse's life and share the joy and sorrow, or you can refuse to open the door and stay outside where you'll always be a stranger. But if you are committed to developing extraordinary relationships, you'll fling that door wide open, run through it, and be a full partaker of life with the mate God has given you.

Routines

Hobbies and interests are not the only sources of pleasure. Routines, remarkably, can greatly enhance pleasure in your family relationships. It's amazing, really, how much a little thing that's regularly done can add to your life. Routines are important because they give a sense of continuity and shared experience. If you have small children, you have probably discovered how they thrive on routine. They want the same story, the same song, and the same goodnight ritual each evening. They are happiest and most secure when their world is routine and predictable.

To some degree, that is true for adults as well. Routines somehow tie us together with those we love. For example, Melanie and I love to have coffee together. We might drink a cup together in the morning, or we might share a cup later in the day. Sometimes we might be having an especially stressful day, and one of us will ask the other, "Would you like a cup of coffee?" We'll brew the coffee, then sit and relax together while we drink it. It's amazing how the tension seems to just evaporate as we share that simple routine.

It doesn't matter what the routine is; it just matters that it's something simple you both enjoy sharing. Maybe it's sitting by the fire with a cup of hot chocolate, or maybe it's letting your spouse sleep late one day a week and then serving breakfast in bed. Maybe your whole family likes to go for a walk after supper each evening. There's just something about those little, tiny routine things that enriches your family relationships. Look for new things to share as a family, and watch the pleasure it brings and the intimacy that develops.

Security

Possessing a sense of security in a relationship yields much pleasure. It is actually quite easy to build this feeling of security in your spouse and children. Anybody can do it! It's as simple as a well-placed compliment or a word of public praise. When my wife cooks an outstanding meal, I make sure to compliment her in front of the whole family. That lets her know that she is appreciated and that all her hard work for the family has not gone unnoticed.

Singling out a child who has accomplished something is a great way to build confidence and security in that child. I like to publicly announce to the rest of the family when one of my children excels. For example, my daughter, Melissa, made nearly a 4.0 in her first semester of college. As the family was gathered together for Thanksgiving, I singled her out, emphasizing what an achievement she had accomplished. I do that with all my children. Of course, they blush a little and look embarrassed, but inwardly that public affirmation brings them much pleasure and develops inward security.

This is one thing most of us don't do nearly often enough. What would your spouse or children think if you gave them a small gift for no apparent reason, just because you appreciate who they are? Can you imagine their pleasure if you were to say, "I just wanted you to know how special you are to me"? They would thrive in that kind of family environment, and your relationship would grow sweeter and sweeter.

It's important in a church, too, to affirm people and build them up. I always like to tell somebody who did something good, "You really did an awesome thing. That was a wonderful thing you did. You surely heard from God." But even if I don't acknowledge someone, God has a way of doing it. I can't possibly know what everyone in my church is doing, but God does, and He singles out and recognizes as He wills.

This point was brought home to me when a woman in the church came up to me and shared what had happened to her. She had decided to help a needy family for Christmas through a program we call Christmas Makers. This woman chose to provide for a single mother who had five children. The family had no money, the mother had no job, and they could not afford to have a Christmas celebration. The woman from the church went and picked up the entire family and brought them to the mall. She bought some clothes for the woman and a toy for each child. When she got to the register to pay for the purchases, she began realizing that she did not have enough money to pay for everything.

It just so happened that one of the Bethany pastors was in the same store at the same time and saw her. He walked up to her and said, "I don't know why, but the Lord has impressed me that you're going to need this." With those words, he wrote a check and handed it to her. When the woman's purchases were totaled, sure enough, she didn't have enough money of her own. She looked at the check the pastor had given her, and it was written for the exact amount she needed! So you see, God saw the good deed this woman was doing and singled her out, causing a pastor to notice and meet her need in an unexpected way.

The story did not end there, however. The single mom felt so blessed and loved by the woman from our church that she, along with her family, attended church, and all of them got saved. The security of knowing that someone cared enough about her to single her out and provide a real Christmas for her children led this unsaved woman to the greatest gift of all: salvation through Jesus!

A Time to Mourn and a Time to Dance

The last portion of the verse in Ecclesiastes 3:4 says that there is "a time to mourn, and a time to dance." When you share the pain of others, you are joining in with their weeping and mourning. When you share their pleasure, you are joining in with their laughing and dancing. I was thinking about that phrase *a time to dance,* and I realized that there is an important distinction between laughing and dancing: laughing is spontaneous, but dancing is planned.

The things that bring the most pleasure to your family are the activities that involve careful planning. The planning of a special activity allows for your family to anticipate the event long before it even happens. Many times the planning and getting ready bring almost as much pleasure as the event itself. There is just something that is so much fun when you are planning and discussing an upcoming vacation and everyone is excited about it.

Have you ever told your children in advance about a vacation that was coming up? If your children are like mine, they probably wore you out with a thousand and one questions before the time of departure ever arrived! But, you see, the pleasure of anticipation was almost more than they could bear.

One year when Christmas rolled around, one of my younger sons was practically beside himself with eager anticipation of the big day. He started asking three days early if he could open his presents. Every day he would have a new way of presenting his request. He just couldn't wait for the time when he could open the presents. Finally, when Christmas morning arrived, he woke up much earlier than anyone else in the family. The sheer anticipation and delight was more than he could stand, so, of course, he had to wake everyone else up, too, and we had to open the presents. He could not wait another moment.

Pleasure builds with anticipation. When you plan something with your family, you all get to share in the fun of getting ready for it as well as actually doing it. Those times bond you together and build a wealth of memories that are uniquely yours as a family. Years later you will recall the fond memories of the time you all went camping or the time the family went to Disney World or whatever special event you planned and executed as a family.

Sometimes you can stumble upon something that brings such pleasure to one of your family members that you can make a special plan to do that activity in a big way. For instance, at Christmas one year, my two youngest boys got paintball guns. Someone came up with the idea that we would play hunter and rabbit. My boys would be the hunters, and I would be the rabbit! We went outside to a large field near our home, and for two hours, I hid behind bushes, scampered into the open, ran just as fast as I could, and did whatever I thought a hunted rabbit would do. Those two boys stalked me for all they were worth. One of them hit me so hard that he practically knocked my helmet off. The other hit me right between the shoulder blades as I was trying to escape. They absolutely screamed with glee. For two solid hours we played, and after it was all over, they just couldn't quit talking about it.

When I saw how much pleasure it brought my two little boys, I decided that we would plan a major outing to the woods where they could hunt me to their hearts' content. That's what I mean by "dancing" in a relationship. Planning times of sheer fun and joy will cement your family bonds like nothing else.

Relationships do not exist within a sterile vacuum. They are not meant to be dull, expressionless, and monotonous. Healthy emotions enhance pleasure and empower; unhealthy emotions squelch joy and destroy. Where there is no weeping, laughing, mourning, or dancing, relationships die; but where there is shared sorrow and joy, you will find a functional family sharing life together in extraordinary relationships.

CHAPTER 3

Extraordinary Intimacy: Innocence in Physical Relationships

There is a physical aspect to the relationships within your family that can be either pure and innocent or tainted and shameful. When God created you, He did not give you just a spirit and emotions, but He housed you within a physical body. That body has physical desires and needs because that's the way God designed it; nevertheless, unless you learn proper boundaries and restraints, you can cause much damage in this important area of your life.

Ecclesiastes 3:5 tells us that there is "a time to embrace, and a time to refrain from embracing." Most Bible scholars agree that this verse is referring to physical contact between the sexes. Healthy physical relationships build you up and restore confidence and security. Negative physical relationships, on the other hand, destroy your sense of self-worth and self-respect. You must, therefore, address this vital component in your relationships.

God's desire for this area of your life is that you have extraordinary physical relationships. He wants your heart healed, your emotions restored, and your physical life innocent. The need for physical touch is God-given and inherent in the heart of every person. In and of itself, it is good; it is only when people distort it that it becomes harmful.

In the 1940s in a London orphanage, a truly remarkable thing was discovered about this need for physical touch. It is a well-known story, but I think it bears repeating. In this orphanage, many of the babies were dying for no apparent reason. They were fed, clothed, and sheltered, but because of understaffing, the babies received very little physical contact other than what was needed to care for them. Someone came up with the idea to simply start touching the babies more. To the surprise and delight of the orphanage staff, the infant mortality rate dropped from 50 percent to 15 percent. The babies, it appeared, had been dying simply from a lack of physical contact. That's how critical this human need is, and that's why I'm addressing the topic.

A Time to Embrace

From the very beginning, God created us for physical intimacy. Look at Genesis 2:21–22: "And the Lord God caused a deep sleep to fall upon Adam, and he slept: and he took one of his ribs, and closed up the flesh instead thereof; And the rib, which the Lord God had taken from man, made he a woman, and brought her unto the man." The word *made* in this passage means "to build" in the Hebrew. God "built" the woman, whereas the man was formed from the dust of the earth. The word *build* is the same word that's used in the Hebrew when referring to building a temple. So God formed Adam from the dust of the earth, then constructed, or built, a woman from his rib. From the very beginning, there was a close, intimate physical relationship between the man and the woman.

Notice also how God brought the woman to the man. It

was His desire that Adam and Eve be in close relationship with each other. From time immemorial, fathers have given their daughters in marriage, and here we find the pattern in Scripture, where God takes Eve and presents her to Adam. Adam recognizes immediately the closeness of the relationship he and Eve are to share as he looks at this lovely creature and says, "This is now bone of my bones, and flesh of my flesh: she shall be called Woman, because she was taken out of Man" (Gen. 2:23). In both English and Hebrew, the word *woman* is a derivative of the word *man*. The woman, though derived from the man, was in every way his equal. He was not complete without her, and she was incomplete without him. That is the way God designed it, and that is the kind of relationship He wants you to have in your marriage.

God placed Adam and Eve in the Garden of Eden, and He specifically created them so that they would complement each other perfectly in every way. That included their physical bodies. This perfect union of man and woman is described in verse 24: "Therefore shall a man leave his father and his mother, and shall cleave unto his wife: and they shall be one flesh." One flesh! That is the union God desires—a oneness that is so complete that the two individuals become like one. It means a perfect union of body, soul, and emotions that is expressed in the context of physical intimacy.

That's why sexual purity is so important. In 1 Corinthians 6:16, Paul tells us that he who joins himself to a harlot becomes one flesh with her. In other words, there is a supernatural, spiritual connection that occurs when intimate physical contact takes place. When occurring within the context of marriage, this union is pure and holy. There is nothing shameful about expressed marital love. In fact, in Genesis 2:25, the Word of God says of Adam and Eve that "they were both naked, the man and his wife, and were not ashamed." They were not ashamed or embarrassed because they were in an innocent, pure relationship that God

Himself had sanctioned. They were one flesh in every sense of the phrase, and their relationship was intimate, healthy, and affirming.

A Time to Refrain from Embracing

Physical intimacy without innocence always brings shame. Innocence is the key word in proper physical relationships. Adam and Eve were innocent in the Garden before the Fall. But after the Fall, they became filled with shame and were embarrassed by their nakedness. They listened to Satan's lie and, as a result, lost their innocence.

Anytime that Satan entices people to enter into improper physical intimacy, shame is always the end result. Take David's illicit relationship with Bathsheba as recorded in the Old Testament. Tremendous shame and heartache came upon David's life as a result of this sin. It led to murder, deception, and ultimately rebellion from his sons. David's entire life was marked by the consequences of his shameful act of adultery with Bathsheba.

We in the United States are living in a sexually charged society where physical intimacy with no covenant relationship is viewed as not only acceptable, but even normal. From radio to television to the movies, sex is a hot topic in most of the entertainment industry. Premarital sex, homosexual behavior, and extramarital affairs are all presented as though they are perfectly acceptable forms of behavior. In fact, many sitcoms on television openly mock those who believe that physical intimacy is something reserved for marriage. We are constantly bombarded with an erroneous view of intimacy as something with no bounds, no standards, and no constraints. Never is the very real danger of sexually transmitted disease raised, and children born out of wedlock are no big deal to those who buy this distorted view of human sexuality.

Don't feed your mind on such garbage from the media, and carefully monitor what your children are watching. Train and teach your family from the Word of God, not from godless sitcoms that glorify sin and deride moral behavior. God wants your physical relationship in your marriage to be innocent, wholesome, and healthy. He wants husband and wife to enjoy each other, and he wants children to receive loving, affirming physical touch from their parents.

There are three main areas of innocence that you've got to maintain if you are going to protect your physical relationships. If you will learn these and guard them in your family, you will experience the joy of extraordinary physical relationships.

Innocence in Family Relationships

God made families to touch! An embrace in the context of innocence within the family is godly. Many of you did not grow up in families that did much hugging, embracing, or kissing. Your family was just not very openly affectionate, so you are somewhat uncomfortable with displays of affection. But it might help you to know that there are several references in the Bible where family relationships were greatly enhanced and strengthened through physical contact.

One of these instances is found in the story of the prodigal son in Luke 15. When the wayward son returned home to his father, the father didn't just slap the boy on his back and grunt. No, look at verse 20: "His father saw him, and had compassion, and ran, and fell on his neck, and kissed him." This was no cool, calm, and collected dad, but a man who ran out to meet his son, grabbed him around the neck, and kissed him joyfully. You see, there is a time and place for displays of affection, and this was one of those times! There was nothing strange or perverted in the father's behavior; it was simply the uncontainable joy of seeing a lost child return.

Children need appropriate physical contact from their parents. The way it is expressed may change as the children grow and mature, but the need for physical contact is never totally gone. When your children are infants, you cuddle them and hold them close to your heart. You stroke their chubby cheeks and touch their tiny toes. It seems you can't stop kissing their sweet little faces. As they grow older, you don't gush over them like you did when they were babies, but you still need to show them physical affection. A good-night kiss, an arm around the shoulder, or a tousle of the hair can all speak volumes to a child.

I remember when my daughter, Melissa, was eighteen and home from college for a holiday. She and I went out with two of her brothers. Her brothers were in the front seat of the car, and Melissa and I were in the back seat. We were all talking and laughing and having a really good time. It was a cold night, so I put my arm around my daughter to keep her warm. And my daughter just snuggled right up to me. I was sitting there, thinking to myself how wonderful it was just to have her near me. It was a special time, and it's the kind of thing all girls need from their fathers. There is nothing more healthy and secure for a daughter than to feel the strength of her father's arm around her.

Maybe it's been a long time since you've hugged your children. Maybe they've disappointed you and let you down, like the prodigal did with his father. But I urge you to reach out to them anyway and give them that warm embrace that says "You're my kid no matter what, and I love you." It could be just the thing to begin breaking down the wall between you and that child and developing a relationship that will truly be extraordinary.

Another story in the Bible that shows healthy physical touch in a family is the story of two brothers, Jacob and Esau. Because of sibling rivalry, parental favoritism, subtle manipulation, and outright deception, the two brothers were estranged for years. Finally, Jacob was returning home and had to face Esau. Not knowing what Esau's reaction would be, Jacob nervously awaited the confrontation. But the Bible records a touching scene of family forgiveness and renewal: "And Esau ran to meet him, and embraced him, and fell on his neck, and kissed him: and they wept" (Gen. 33:4). In that moment of warm embrace, the two brothers were knit together again—brothers in heart as well as flesh.

Yet a third story shows us again the healing power of touch in a family situation. You probably remember the story of Joseph, sold by his brothers into slavery in Egypt, imprisoned in that foreign land, and then finally released and put into a position of high honor. Despite the horrendous betrayal suffered at the hands of his own brothers, Joseph, twenty years later when reunited with his brothers, was overcome with emotion, kissing his brothers and weeping profusely over them (Gen. 45:14–15). The family was reconciled, forgiveness was granted, and relationships were restored.

Physical affection is so vital in healthy family relationships, but so many of us have a hard time with it. Part of the reason, I believe, is our independent American culture. We want our space, and we don't want anyone to trespass upon it. It's not like that in much of the rest of the world, however. In Latin America, families are very expressive, hugging and showing much affection. In Africa, where I lived for a couple of years as a missionary, it's that way, too. It's even that way in Russia and some of the eastern European nations.

As a college student, I went behind the Iron Curtain in 1974 and was caught off guard, to say the least, when a Romanian pastor grabbed me and kissed me on the cheek. My natural tendency was to pull away and say, "Back off, dude!" But he was just expressing his joy at having us as visitors. I think we in America could learn a thing or two from other nations. We tend to be stiff, starchy, and reserved when it comes to physical touch, whereas people in many other places have learned the potential for closeness that is inherent in physical contact.

You can take this thought and use it to make a tremendous difference with your family members. Start today to show affection to them. It doesn't matter if no one else does it—you be the different one. You be the one who puts the arm around their shoulders and says, "Hey, how are you? What's going on?" They may look at you like you've lost your mind, but give them time and keep doing it, and they will respond. There is something so bonding and so healing in simply expressing open affection in a family.

One caution that must be made is that it is extremely important to maintain innocence in your expression of physical touch. Obviously, some people have abused that and have caused much trauma and pain because of their inappropriate behavior. Never, when showing physical affection to a child, are you allowed to do anything that is questionable or even hints of sexual overtones. The purity and innocence of the family must be maintained at all costs, or the results are disastrous.

In 2 Samuel 13, Amnon, son of King David, committed incest with his half-sister, Tamar, against her will. He raped her and then rejected her, destroying her chance of any kind of life in Israel. Tamar's brother, Absalom, harbored a seething hatred against Amnon for his vile act, and two years later he took his revenge and had his brother killed. That may sound extreme to you, but there is no end to the lives that have been wrecked and the families torn apart because of a loss of innocence in physical relationships.

Innocence in Marriage Relationships

In the relationship between husband and wife, God ordained healthy, fulfilling sexual union. God created Eve for Adam and Adam for Eve. They were to become one flesh, and their bodies were perfectly designed so that physical union could occur. Sexual relations, as God ordained it, is a very beautiful thing. It is meant to be a physical expression of deep love and commitment between husband and wife. This physical union can occur naturally only between the sexes, not within them. That is what makes homosexual relations so wrong. That type of sexual expression is not a reflection of the complementary male and female bodies, but rather a perversion of God's original design for the sexual expression of love.

God does all things perfectly, and His plan for sexual fulfillment does not have an alternative expression—no matter how many people with political clout try to say otherwise. Homosexual expression degrades the dignity that God bestowed upon man and woman within their roles in marriage. People were not created to express their sexuality in that way, and when they do, they violate the bonds of innocence in physical relationships, bringing shame and fear to those who participate in it. God, of course, loves homosexuals and desires to set them free, just like He desires to liberate the drunkard, the drug addict, or the glutton. But like any other sinner, the homosexual must first lay down his sin, come to the cross, and receive the forgiveness so freely offered.

Men and women are not only physically different, but they are also emotionally different. This is important to understand because it sheds light on how to maintain sexual purity within marriage. For men, sexual stimulation begins with the eyes. Jesus alluded to this in Matthew 5:28 when He said, "Whosoever looketh on a woman to lust after her hath committed adultery with her already in his heart." He knew the effect of just looking at a woman in an improper fashion. That's why it is so vital for men to guard their eyes. I recommend to all men to do as Job 31:1 NIV says: "I made a covenant with my eyes not to look lustfully at a girl."

The eye brings instant stimulation to a man, and once an erotic image is painted on the mind, it's extremely difficult to erase. A man cannot afford to think that just one glance won't hurt anything. By his very nature, a man is weak in this area and must remain diligent if he is not to fall into the devil's trap. Men, you must guard the "eye gate" and refuse to indulge in anything pornographic or inappropriate. Put a filter on your computer, and monitor carefully what comes into your home from television or videos. At all costs, flee from lewdness, lust, and anything impure. Resist fiercely every temptation to engage in anything questionable, and make yourself accountable to another man for sexual purity.

Unlike the man, the woman is not generally stimulated through the eye, but rather through the ear. For her, stimulation comes from what she hears. Many women are busy at home and have the television on as they go about their daily tasks. Although they may not be sitting down and watching, they are listening as they do the ironing or the cleaning, and they can tell you what they heard. If men realize this about their wives, they can use that knowledge to foster intimacy.

Husband, your wife is waiting for you to talk to her! She wants you to tell her something romantic or to share your deepest thoughts and feelings with her. She wants to hear you say, "Baby, you're wonderful. You are so beautiful. I don't know what I would do without you." That's what she wants to hear! When you affirm her with words, it makes her feel secure and protected. She is waiting to hear you talk to her.

Both husband and wife have to be aware of each other's needs. If both concentrate on meeting the needs of the other, the marriage will flourish in all aspects, including the physical relationship. The husband must make a genuine effort to speak in an uplifting fashion that makes his wife feel cherished. When she is hearing complimentary words of praise and appreciation, she is much more likely to be sexually responsive. And the wife, in turn, must remember her husband's attraction through the eyes. That means, ladies, watch what you wear to bed at night! Some of you wear flannel from head to toe all four seasons of the year. Others of you wear the same T-shirt that you've been sleeping in since high school. You need to be stimulating physically to your husband, remembering that what he sees is going to have a big impact on him. When both husband and wife are focused on giving each other pleasure through the ways that are meaningful to each of them, the marriage will move to a higher level of intimacy and sexual fulfillment.

Just as you must be so careful to maintain proper boundaries in your physical relationships with your children, you must also be sure to protect those boundaries between the sexes. Women, knowing that men receive stimulation through the eye, must be careful in how they present themselves. Modesty and proper decorum are paramount. Provocative, revealing clothing has no place in public for the Christian woman. She must guard how she presents herself to the opposite sex. Men, too, must guard how they act around women other than their wives. They have no right to flirt and talk intimately to other women. They've got to remember the influence of their words and guard their tongues and what they say to other women. If a married couple will respect proper boundaries with the opposite sex, they will protect their marriage from outside temptations and will foster a truly extraordinary relationship.

Innocence in Dating Relationships

The issue of purity in dating relationships is another issue that must be addressed. A large percentage of America is unmarried, and many young people today are waiting longer to get married. As a result, many people are remaining single for longer periods, and they have to make a decision about how they are going to conduct themselves in relationships with the opposite sex.

Despite what popular culture portrays, it is possible to have godly, pure relationships during the time that you are unmarried. Television and movies make it seem like you are just a victim of uncontrollable passion, but that is not the truth! You don't have to go from one relationship to another, giving away your heart and innocence time after time, only to be hurt over and over again. No, there is a better way. You can have extraordinary dating relationships if you will commit yourself to following a few basic guidelines from the Word of God.

God intends for your relationships to be strengthening and empowering, not debilitating and destructive. He has established certain boundaries to protect you, and if you will obey Him in how you conduct yourself in relationships with the opposite sex, you will be able to maintain your innocence. Never forget that once you lose your innocence, it's gone forever. You cannot get it back. It is such a sacred thing to give yourself physically to someone, and for that reason, it must be reserved for marriage.

In 1 Corinthians 7, Paul gives some instructions for maintaining sexual purity in relationships. First, he addresses the sexual union between husband and wife, admonishing them to maintain a consistent physical relationship and not to routinely deny each other physical affection (vv. 2–5). Then, he moves his discussion to the unmarried. In verse 7, he says that he wishes everyone could be as he is and not have to marry, but then he goes on to say that this is a gift that not everyone has.

That's right—singleness can be a gift from God! Some people never marry because they have no great need to. They are content and fulfilled being single, and actually, they have a distinct spiritual advantage in serving God, since they are not hindered by family duties or responsibilities, like married people are. The single person is in a unique position to serve God wholeheartedly without limitation. So if God calls you to be single, that is a good thing. Society may try to tell you that you are strange or odd, but the Word of God says it is a gift.

Some people are single, however, not because it is their gift, but because they haven't yet met the right person. The Word of God provides guidance here, too. In 1 Corinthians 7:8–9 NIV Paul says, "Now to the unmarried and the widows I say: It is good for them to stay unmarried, as I am. But if they cannot control themselves, they should marry, for it is better to marry than to burn with passion." If you are currently single but desire to marry, you are going to have to answer the question of what to do with your physical desires and passions. In other words, self-control is going to be a big issue for you. But, I believe, if you will take a few commonsense precautions and if you will submit yourself to God and His standard, you will be successful in this area.

Let me start by saying that if you are currently single, relax! There is nothing wrong with you just because you are not married, and in fact, it is so much better to be unmarried than to be married to the wrong person. Most of us know people who just had to get married and took the first person that came along; inevitably, they live to regret it. So if you are single, just be patient and maintain godliness in your relationships while you wait on the Lord to bring the right one along. Devote yourself totally to Him, and refuse the stigma that others try to attach to you for being single.

As you develop your relationship with God and wait on Him to bring the right person to you, there are some practical steps you can take to maintain purity in your dating relationships. They may not be popular, and they may run counter to what society and others have told you, but if you will follow these guidelines, you can save yourself a lot of trouble and heartache. First and foremost, establish in your heart the principle that there is no place for physical intimacy within the context of dating. If you embrace this principle right off the top, you will have a foundation to protect you in tempting situations.

If you are single but dating, you should submit your relationships to parents and spiritual leaders. They can be more objective about a potential mate than can you, and they have your best interest at heart. It is the wise young man or woman who will submit a relationship to parents and follow their godly instruction. If your parents approve of the relationship and you are progressing towards marriage, then you need to go through premarriage counseling and prepare for a true covenant marriage.

Even if you are dating a person that you plan to marry, you still have no right to cross physical boundaries of propriety. The boundaries should be strict and narrow because once you start pushing back the boundaries, you start compromising your standards of purity more and more. I counsel dating couples to maintain total innocence and accountability in their relationship. Kissing, petting, and embracing are all parts of Satan's plan to cause you to lose your innocence. Refrain from any physical expressions of love or affection.

I know that sounds ridiculous and puritanical to some of you, but once you move into the physical arena in a relationship, you lose objectivity about the person. Once the physical senses are aroused, you begin focusing on that and ignoring the greater issues of finances, background, callings, and areas of potential problems. Your relationship becomes colored by what you are experiencing physically.

It's a lie from Satan that you've got to see if you are compatible with someone before you can marry. If you reserve physical expressions until you marry, no one is going to have to teach you what to do! Believe me, you'll know what to do when the time comes. But if you arouse the physical senses before the time for their expression has arrived, you are playing with fire. It will always take you further than you intended to go, and shame results when you cross boundaries of physical intimacy.

So when you are dating someone, decide ahead of time that you are going to remain completely pure in the relationship. There is no such thing as being too pure in a dating relationship; you don't need to do anything of a physical nature. You don't have to give a goodnight kiss, and you don't even have to hold hands. You don't have to hug and caress, and you certainly don't have the right of sexual expression. Just decide all those issues in your mind right now.

When physical intimacy is not a part of your dating relationship, then you are free to develop the emotional and spiritual aspects. You maintain your respect and dignity, and you can ask the questions that are truly important. Start with the question of whether or not the person you are seeing truly knows the Lord. If the answer is no, then you have no business being in the relationship. If you overlook that most basic starting point and say, "Oh, I'll get him (her) saved after we get married," then you are treading in very dangerous waters. The Bible tells us specifically, "Be ye not unequally yoked together with unbelievers: for what fellowship hath righteousness with unrighteousness? and what communion hath light with darkness?" (2 Cor. 6:14).

You have nothing in common with an unsaved person, and you have no business getting involved in a serious dating relationship with someone who doesn't know the Lord. Furthermore, if you do marry an unsaved person, you have no guarantee that he or she will get saved. The Scriptures say it clearly: "For how do you know, O wife, whether you will save your husband? Or how do you know, O husband, whether you will save your wife?" (1 Cor. 7:16 NKJV).

When you enter a dating relationship, always start with the question of whether or not the person is saved. If you can answer yes to that, then ask these questions: Does the person have integrity? Does he have inner character? Can I trust his word? Has he lied to me? Does he know how to manage finances? Does he tithe? How does he feel about children? Is he considerate, kind, and loving? And the list could include many other such questions, of course.

If the relationship progresses with your parents' approval to the stage of engagement, then you need to commit to premarital counseling. At our church, we will not marry just anybody. You can't show up and say, "I want to get married tomorrow" and expect us to marry you. We take marriage as a very serious trust, and before we will marry you, we want to make sure that it is right and in the will of God. We require engaged couples to go through three months of premarital counseling, where we cause them to address issues that could lead to problems in marriage.

There is great protection for the young person who will submit his choice of a marriage partner first to his parents and then to the church. It is not God's intent for young people to just go out into the world, experiment with the opposite sex, and then choose anybody they feel like they might want to marry. Young people should not be sleeping around and losing their innocence, bringing children into the world that they are ill prepared to care for. Young people should be listening to their parents and seeking godly counsel concerning their dating relationships. They should wait until they receive their parents' blessing before proceeding to marriage. That way, they will have every advantage and possibility of having a marriage that is truly extraordinary.

Restoring Innocence in Relationships

I have described the ideal in our family, marriage, and dating relationships. Although we should always strive for the highest standard possible, we all fall short. There is not a one of us that has had a perfect life with perfect innocence in everything.

When people lose their innocence, they are deeply ashamed and try to hide or cover up the guilt and embarrassment they feel. When Adam and Eve sinned in the Garden, they lost their innocence and realized for the first time that they were naked. In an attempt to cover their shame, they sewed fig leaves to make clothing (Gen. 3:7). Their shame deepened, and they tried to hide from God (v. 9). God, of course, knew what they had done and called them out of hiding. He knew the shame they were feeling. They had disobeyed God, rebelled, eaten of the fruit, and, consequently, were full of shame and self-reproach. They had lost their innocence, and there they were, running around in those silly little fig leaves they had sewn together.

What a picture that is of religion! Religion, without the presence of the living God, can only attempt to make people feel better by offering empty platitudes. Religion has nothing to offer to bring release and peace to those who have lost their innocence. Relationship with God, however, reconciles even the filthiest, vilest sinner through the blood that Jesus shed on the cross.

Only by the shedding of blood is there remission of sins, and we see this truth first set forth in Genesis 3. In verse 21, God made Adam and Eve clothes of skin to replace the fig leaves they had used to try to cover themselves. In order for there to be skins, there had to be the death of an animal, and the death of an animal was accompanied by the shedding of blood.

I'm sure there must have been blood on the underside of those skins that God placed around Adam and Eve, but He wrapped them in the skins anyway. I can just imagine Him saying, "I know you're feeling shame. I know you're feeling fear and condemnation. Here, let me put this around you." And then He enveloped them in the cloaks of skin, with the shed blood covering them, thus signifying the necessity of the shedding of blood to atone for sins.

From that point on, the entire system of sacrifice in the Old Testament was based upon the shedding of the blood of animals. Thousands of animals had to be slaughtered, but their blood could only cover sin; it had no power to cleanse or erase the sinful past. But in the New Testament, we read, "For if the blood of bulls and of goats, and the ashes of an heifer sprinkling the unclean, sanctifieth to the purifying of the flesh: How much more shall the blood of Christ, who through the eternal Spirit offered himself without spot to God, purge your conscience from dead works to serve the living God?" (Heb. 9:13–14). The blood of Christ cleanses our consciences because it completely atones for all our sins!

When Jesus died on the cross of Calvary, the final blood sacrifice was offered. The blood of animals could never bring atonement for sin, but when Christ, the spotless Lamb, was crucified, the blood debt for all humanity was paid in full. Only His blood has the power to cancel all vestiges of sin and to cleanse you totally. It doesn't matter what is in your past, how you lost your innocence, or how horrible was the sin. No matter what you have done, the cross of Christ and the blood of Jesus can cleanse your heart and conscience. He can make you as white as the driven snow (Isa. 1:18) and remove your sin as far from you as the east is from the west (Ps. 103:12).

Years ago Brother Danny Ost, a great missionary to Mexico, related the touching story of a prostitute who had been with many men. One glorious day, however, she was saved, delivered, and set free, and the Osts brought her into their home to live with them. This young woman was overflowing with joy in her new life. She enrolled in Bible school and met a young man there. The two fell in love and planned to marry. Everything seemed to be going great, the wedding date was set, and everyone was so excited with the upcoming celebration. Then one day someone informed Brother Danny that the young woman was upstairs in her room, crying bitterly. Danny and his wife, Ruby, went upstairs to the young girl and asked her what was wrong. Heartbroken, she replied, "I'm getting married, and I can't wear white because I have been with so many men in my life." She had lost her innocence and was now so grieved because cultural tradition allowed only virgins to wear white at their weddings.

Brother Danny went to his room to pray about the situation. The Lord reminded him of the marriage supper of the Lamb and the words in Revelation 19:7–8 that say we will all be clothed in fine white linen at the marriage feast. Brother Danny went back to the young lady and said, "You are covered in the blood of Jesus, and if He clothes you in white linen for His marriage supper, then you're certainly clean enough to be married in white here in Mexico." Brother Danny knew that although the young lady was a former prostitute, she was totally cleansed by the blood of Jesus. When she came to Christ, her lost innocence was restored, and God saw her as a totally new creation, pure and untainted.

God is no respecter of persons. What He does for one of His children, He'll do for the next. You may have committed acts that you are deeply ashamed of, or you may have had things done to you against your will. Regardless of what has happened in your life, God can restore your innocence. He can wash you clean of every stain of sin and give you a second chance at living a life of innocence.

If you have lost your innocence in any way, God is waiting to restore it to you. Come to the cross, admit your sin, ask for the blood to cleanse your conscience, and then go forward into extraordinary physical relationships. That's what the Great Physician prescribes!

CHAPTER 4

Extraordinary Finances: Being a Steward in God's Kingdom

All of us on this earth have stuff! Some of us have more than others, but we all possess something. In fact, the accumulation of material things is the sole focus in life for many people. They want more things and will do anything to acquire more money, more gadgets, a sportier car, or a larger house. In the process, unfortunately, they often run roughshod over anyone who gets in their way, including those they should most cherish—their families. If possessions or money is your primary motivation, you will sacrifice your family on the altar of greed and mammon. On the other hand, if you learn how to be a wise steward of your resources and balance this with your family responsibilities, you will be one of the few to truly live in the blessing of extraordinary relationships.

Ecclesiastes 3:6 says that there is "a time to get, and a time to lose; a time to keep, and a time to cast away." That verse, among other things, is referring to your finances. When you learn the balance between getting things and letting go of them, and between gathering to yourself and discarding of what you don't need, the quality of your relationships will be affected positively. That's because you can't divorce money and finances from the rest of your life. Your finances are an integral part of your family life, and you've got to learn how to manage them properly, or you will cause great havoc in your home.

Ownership or Stewardship?

The concept of stewardship rather than ownership can change your life! It is an idea, however, that goes contrary to what most of us have been taught. We live in a world of "ownership." We feel that we have the right to own everything we manage to possess. It's a humanistic philosophy that says, "I'm the master of my own fate. I earned this money. I was smart enough to make it, and I can spend it however I choose. Whatever I buy belongs to me. It's mine, and no one else has a right to it, because I own it." That type of philosophy, however, is diametrically opposed to the Word of God.

Psalm 24:1 says, "The earth is the Lord's, and the fulness thereof; the world, and they that dwell therein." Everything—absolutely everything—belongs to God, and we possess nothing. We are simply stewards of whatever God entrusts to us. The world cannot understand this type of philosophy, but to those of us who have been born anew into God's family, it is divine revelation to direct us in the use of our worldly resources. When we get saved, the question changes from "What should I do with *my* money?" to "God, what do You want me to do with *Your* money?"

That might sound like a scary proposition to you—to let God have complete control over all your earthly possessions—but in reality, He owns it all anyway. You can't really give anything back to Him, because it's already His!

When you realize that you are just a steward, or a manager, of your earthly possessions, it takes all the pressure off of you. You can relax and entrust all your things to God, because they really don't belong to you anyway.

It's kind of like this: If you're driving your car and somebody backs into it, you will probably get upset or angry. It's *your* car that was damaged, and you don't like it. But if you are in a company car and somebody dents it a little, it doesn't bother you all that much. The car isn't your car; you are just an employee of the company that owns it. So you just go to your supervisor and say, "Somebody backed into my car. Can you fix it?" And he does.

When you grasp the fact that God owns everything you have, you realize that He is responsible to take care of it. He has the right to do whatever He wants with your possessions, but He also bears the responsibility of providing for you. When you know that the Lord is your shepherd, then you have the assurance that you shall not want. The two go hand in hand. That's the confidence that comes from knowing that God is the owner of everything and you are just a steward.

I heard a story that helps explain this point of God being your provider. During World War II, there were a great many orphans in Europe, and camps were built to house them. The children were well provided for, with a place to sleep and ample food. But the children, it was discovered, were unable to sleep at night because they were afraid that they would have no food the next day.

Someone came up with an ingenious way to get the children to sleep. Before the children went to bed for the evening, they were each given a piece of bread, which they were told to hold on to. They were instructed not to eat the bread, just to hold on to it until the next day. Interestingly, all the orphans began sleeping through the night. They knew that if nothing else, they would have at least that one piece of bread to eat for the next day.

I thought about that story and how it relates to us. You may not have financial security for fifty years from now, but the same God who "put the bread in your hand" today will give it to you tomorrow. He is your provider, and He will take care of you. All the resources of the earth belong to Him, and He delights to share them with you one day at a time. Knowing that, you can have peace and face any financial situation with the assurance that God is there for you.

A Christian lives by faith, and acknowledging that all your possessions belong to God will help you to live by faith in Him as provider. You don't own your life or anything in it; it all belongs to God. When you die and go to heaven, you will receive your eternal reward and inheritance, but while you are on this earth, you possess nothing.

I like the way John Wesley viewed it. When his house burned down, it is reported that he stood there watching the smoldering flames and remarked, "The Lord's house has burned. One less responsibility for me." What a testimony of faith! John Wesley knew that God would take care of him, and he didn't have to worry about it. Knowing that will bring you extraordinary peace and grace in the most difficult situations.

Stuff or Relationships?

Money is only a tool. It is neither positive nor negative. It can be used to either build relationships or destroy them. Money does not bring happiness. Freedom, health, and rewarding relationships are the things that bring true happiness. But you are going to have to decide if you really believe that. You are going to have to ask yourself, "Am I going to focus on stuff, or will I focus on relationships?"

Your possessions and your relationships, ideally, should be kept in balance, like a seesaw. But what happens far too often in our American culture is that the seesaw becomes unbalanced, with material possessions having far too much weight in our lives. Most of us are drowning in material things. We work more hours to earn more money to buy more stuff to cram into our closets, attics, and garages. Some of us have to add on to our houses in order to accommodate all the stuff we own! We have built our lives around things rather than relationships, and the more we focus on stuff, the less we focus on relationships. When money is king, then we really don't think about our relationships at all. That's just the way it works.

When you come to Christ, however, the seesaw should come back into balance and relationships with God, family, and the community should now be the most important factors in your life. Life is all about relationships, not money and material things. Jesus said, "But seek ye first the kingdom of God, and his righteousness; and all these things shall be added unto you" (Matt. 6:33). "These things" refers to material necessities and possessions, as mentioned earlier in Matthew 6. God knows you need such things, but the pursuit of them was never meant to be the goal of life.

When "stuff" is your highest priority, your relationships will automatically suffer. You might not think so, but it really is true. One or the other is going to take precedence in your life. If a man is focused primarily on making money, he is going to work as much overtime as he can, even when it means he misses his kids' ball games and dance recitals. He promises to go next time, but of course, "next time" never comes. He is always too busy making money to be involved in the lives of his children or wife. Consequently, his relationships suffer, and the price he pays for earning more money is higher than he ever dreamed.

I don't know how many tragic stories I have heard from kids whose parents have given them everything except what they most wanted: a close, warm relationship. These kids tell me they hate their parents, and when I ask them why, they say, "My parents have never had any time for me. They work so much that I never see them." When these kids turn eighteen, they head for the door and life on their own because they have nothing to hold them at home.

It's the same in a marriage. If a man works, works, works, but never spends time with his wife, he is in real danger of losing her. I've seen husbands who have worked their heads off, only to come home one day and find a note that says, "I'm leaving." Shocked and bewildered, the husband wonders why. Thinking he gave his wife everything, he fails to realize he neglected to give her the one thing she really wanted: a relationship with him.

Only a truly wise person understands the value of relationships over material goods. In Scripture, we see how a woman (some say it was Mary Magdalene) took a very expensive perfume and poured it upon the feet of Jesus (Matt. 26:7–13). Judas was present at this lavish display of love and devotion and got very upset, saying the perfume should have been sold and the money given to the poor. His emphasis was on the value of the perfume (a year's salary), rather than on the relationship that the woman had with Jesus. To her, the cost of the perfume meant nothing; the relationship to Jesus meant everything. To Judas, stuff was more important than relationship, as evidenced in his reaction to the woman's act of love and in his later betrayal of Jesus for a pittance of thirty pieces of silver.

Like Judas, many people continue to deceive themselves, thinking money is all-important. I heard of an Internet survey that asked people what it would take to make them happy. Seventy percent of the respondents said they would be happy if they made another $150 per month! They think a little bit more money is going to bring them happiness, but if they got that little bit, they would just want more. That's human nature: to want more, to be striving for more, yet never realizing that happiness can never be found in money and material possessions.

So many people (including some Christians!) think they would be happy if they could just win the lottery. But those who have won large sums of money often testify of the troubles brought on by it. The happiness they thought the money would bring evaporates as family, friends, and complete strangers try to get a little piece of the pie. Money alone can never fill the void in the human heart. Only relationship with God and relationships with others can do that.

The amount of money you possess does not determine your true wealth. You can be the richest person on earth without having a great deal of money. If you have your freedom, you are rich. So many people all over the world live under repressive political regimes that deny them the most basic liberties. If you live in the United States, however, you are free to travel, to work where you want, to buy a home, to worship God, to protest political injustice, to have as many children as you want, and to live your life in peace. Those are rights so basic that most of us don't even think about them, but millions of people live without what we take for granted. Think about those who are imprisoned, some of them wrongly. What good does all the money in the world do if you are locked in a jail cell somewhere? Freedom is a priceless treasure, and you are truly rich if you are blessed enough to have it.

Another thing that makes you rich in the truest sense of the word is having your health. Most of us don't appreciate our bodies until something goes wrong, but when we get well, we are so appreciative of having a healthy body again. Not everyone has that. You can be a millionaire, but all that money can't cure you of terminal cancer or some other deadly disease. Health is a very precious possession, and no amount of money can guarantee it.

Finally, in addition to freedom and health, relationships bring true happiness and richness to life. The Lord wants you to have extraordinary relationships in your life. If you have no one who loves you and no one for you to love, then all the money in the world is not going to bring you happiness. There is something innate within each of us that craves human connection.

A few years ago there was a movie called *Cast Away* that aptly illustrated this need for relationship. In the movie, the lead character was in a plane crash and ended up on a deserted island. As he began learning to survive on his own, he one day discovered a Wilson volleyball that had been on the plane when it went down. The man was so lonely and hungry for a relationship that he took the ball and transformed it into an imaginary friend. He put eyes on it and drew a nose and a mouth. He took coconut strands and gave his friend some hair. He did everything he could to make the ball look like a human being. He even named his new friend—Wilson.

Wilson became the man's friend and companion for the next several years. During that time, the man talked to the ball, got angry at the ball, asked the ball for its opinion, and developed a relationship with this imaginary companion. Finally, when the man was leaving the island on a makeshift raft, Wilson fell overboard, and the castaway lost his friend. He was heartbroken because that ball was the only thing he had had a relationship with in all those years on the island.

Of course, that was only a movie, but I think it makes a valid point. People must have relationships. No man is an island, and you were never meant to go through this life alone. Money will not bring you richness and fulfillment in life; only relationships with people you love and who love you can do that.

The Bible gives us several examples that illustrate the futility of trying to find happiness in money. In Luke 12:15–21, Jesus told a parable about a rich man who had so much wealth that he had to build bigger barns to contain all his stuff. This guy was ready to retire, had money coming out of his ears, and a bright future ahead of him. What he didn't know was that all his wealth was for nothing because that night his soul would be required of him. This man had bought into the lie that so many people believe: the denial of their own mortality. Many people live with no thought for tomorrow and simply ignore the fact that one day they will die. Death, however, is an inescapable fact of life.

When you lay your head upon your pillow each night, you really don't know if you will wake to see another day. If you are living for money and things, everything you have will all go to someone else when you die. You will have toiled for something temporal that has no lasting value. The old saying "You can't take it with you" is so true. Have you ever seen a U-haul connected to the back of a hearse? Of course not! That's because when this life is over, you are stripped bare of everything, and all your money and fine possessions are left behind for others.

Luke 16:19–31 records another parable. In this story, there was a man who was wealthy and lived in luxury. Another man, Lazarus, was sick and diseased, lying at the rich man's gate, hoping for any kind of mercy. Both men died, with Lazarus going to heaven and the rich man to hell. Though Lazarus had had no material wealth on earth, he now had the full richness of heaven. The rich man, on the other hand, had lived an earthly life of luxury, never giving thought to eternity. He had bought into another common lie: there is no hell. That's what the devil tells people. He says, "Go ahead and live for today. Indulge yourself and enjoy life, because this time on earth is all you have. There's no such place as hell. There's nothing but this life in the here and now."

If you believe that, then you're just like the man in the parable. You are gambling everything on the belief that there is nothing past this earthly life. Faith in God and in a life after death cannot be proven or disproven scientifically.

It belongs to the realm of the spirit. But you are going to have to choose what you are going to believe. I like the way the seventeenth-century philosopher Blaise Pascal explained it: If you choose to believe that there is a God and an afterlife and you end up being wrong, you lose nothing. But if you elect to believe there is no God or eternity and you are wrong, then you lose everything.

The third person in the Scriptures who valued money over relationship was the rich young ruler. In Luke 18:18, he asks Jesus, "What must I do to inherit eternal life?" Eternal life! Nothing is more important than that. To have an immortal body that never grows old, to quench your thirst from the river of life, to eat your fill from the tree of life, and to enjoy forever fellowship with God—nothing could be better than that. And the young man wanted to know how to obtain it.

The Lord answers the rich young ruler's question by first reminding him of the Ten Commandments, to which the man responds, "All these have I kept from my youth up" (v. 21). Jesus counters by telling him that he still lacks one thing: "Sell all that thou hast, and distribute unto the poor, and thou shalt have treasure in heaven: and come, follow me" (v. 22).

Jesus knew how important this man's stuff was to him, and He was giving him an opportunity to make an adjustment in his life and prioritize what was truly important. He was issuing an invitation to the rich young ruler to enter into a relationship with Him, the King of Kings and Lord of Lords, but the man was so wrapped up in material things that he couldn't accept the offer. Instead, he "was very sorrowful: for he was very rich" (v. 23).

Another person in the New Testament who had to resolve the tension between the riches of this world and relationship with Jesus was Zacchaeus. Zacchaeus, if you remember the story, was a wealthy tax collector, and one day when he heard that Jesus was passing by, he climbed a tree so that he could get a better view of Jesus. As the story unfolds, Jesus passes by and calls Zacchaeus down from the tree, saying, "Zacchaeus, make haste, and come down; for today I must abide at thy house" (Luke 19:5). Zacchaeus joyfully responds and tells Jesus, "Behold, Lord, the half of my goods I give to the poor; and if I have taken anything from any man by false accusation, I restore him fourfold" (v. 8).

Look what happened to Zacchaeus! When Jesus called him, Zacchaeus immediately responded, and suddenly his worldly wealth meant nothing to him. He had spent his life accumulating stuff, but when he met Jesus, the entire focus of his life instantly changed. Money now meant so little to him that he decided to give half of his wealth away. That's a big gift, needless to say. But he went even further and said he was going to restore fourfold to anyone he had cheated. Zacchaeus discovered what was really important, and when he did, money lost its hold on him.

Relationships are all that really matters; money is useless in the long term. Remember the timeless story of the prodigal son? When the wayward child returned home after squandering his inheritance, the father said not one word about money. He didn't berate the boy, though he certainly deserved it. He didn't say, "Well, it's about time you came to your senses. You wasted all that money, and I want you to pay back every dime." No, he did nothing of the sort. The money lost was irrelevant to the father, and all that mattered to him was restoring the relationship with his son. He was filled with compassion for the prodigal, and he ran out to meet him, kissing and embracing him. Not only did he receive his son back into the family with total forgiveness, but he also spared no expense to celebrate the son's homecoming. He clothed him with the best robe, put rings upon his fingers, and prepared a splendid feast on his behalf. He didn't care how much it cost him; all he cared about was having his boy home again.

Seeing your children and other family members get saved is worth more than any amount of money. Restoring relationships that have been broken is priceless. If you've been squabbling over a family inheritance, make peace before your relationships are permanently damaged. No material thing is worth losing a relationship over. If you've been begrudging how much money you've been spending on an ungrateful child, just lay that bitterness down and do what is best for the relationship.

Money without relationships is meaningless. Its sole purpose past paying the bills is to foster relationships and further God's kingdom. Don't use your money as a weapon, but as a tool to bless your family and others. Hold lightly to it; never let it gain an importance in your life that it was not meant to have. Use it to influence relationships toward God. That's the ultimate purpose of money.

Money Out of Balance

When material wealth gets out of balance in your life, you will notice one of three things happening, or any combination of them.

Stress

The first thing you will notice in your life is the presence of stress. A marriage can be going along fine, but when money problems hit, the marriage can be sorely tested if the partners don't know how to resolve the conflict. Wives begin accusing their husbands of not being good providers, and husbands go on the defensive and call their wives "shopaholics."

Recent polls have shown that in 57 percent of all divorces, financial problems are the primary cause. That should set off some alarm bells in your head. If money problems can lead to such disastrous consequences, then maybe you'd better sit down with your spouse and start discussing your finances. Maybe it's time to come up with a mutually acceptable plan of spending, investing, getting out of debt, and providing education for your children. A great deal of stress will be automatically eliminated if you can come into agreement with your spouse about how to handle your money.

Sometimes the problem in a marriage isn't a lack of money, but the fact that Dad or Mom or even both have become workaholics. All they do is work, work, work, trying to earn yet another dollar. They may make a lot of money, but the price is high. Not only do they suffer physical stress from working too much and not resting and relaxing enough, but they also soon drift apart in their family relationships. They have time for nothing except making money, and often they don't wake up to the fact that they have destroyed their marriage or their relationships with their kids until it is too late.

Hurt

Money, improperly used or emphasized, can also bring great hurt. People can get very offended in a family when the focus is on who got what and "Why did they get it instead of me?" How many families have been torn apart because of hurt feelings over the disposal of a family inheritance? People can get downright nasty about stuff that doesn't even matter. So what if Susie got Grandma's chest of drawers? You didn't have room for it anyway. It's not worth losing your relationship with your brothers or sisters because they got something you wanted. It's all going to burn one day, and you won't care who got the china and who got the television.

Another thing that can bring much hurt in the area of finances is co-signing a loan. Proverbs 22:26–27 warns, "Be not thou one of them that strike hands, or of them that are sureties for debts. If thou hast nothing to pay, why should he take away thy bed from under thee?" That means don't sign a loan for anyone, including your children. Now, that's hard for most of us. We naturally want to help our kids, but it really is better not to go down that path. Statistics reveal that 50 percent of people who co-sign through a bank end up having to make payments, and 75 percent of those who co-sign through a finance company end up having to pay. Those are pretty sobering statistics.

If you co-sign a loan for a friend or a relative and the person cannot make the payments, you will have to assume responsibility for the notes. Are you prepared for that, not just financially but also emotionally? How will you feel when that "best friend" of yours is riding around in the car that you're paying for because he got mad and quit his job? Can you handle that? You don't want to get into that kind of situation. You don't want to have to pay someone else's debt, but more importantly, you don't want to see a relationship turn sour because of a financial entanglement.

Anger

A third thing that can manifest in relationships where money is being misused is anger. There may be someone in the family who overspends, and anger and tension result. Maybe the person is a gambler, and that can certainly escalate the anger level in the family. I've read that the average person in our country spends $1,174 per year on gambling! Can you believe it? Throwing hard-earned money away, all in the hope of striking it rich! Sad but true, even some Christians are involved in gambling. They give maybe $20 a year to missions, but spend over $1,000 a year at the casino! Some people even get addicted to gambling and lose their homes and retirement funds because of their uncontrollable urge to gamble. You can imagine the anger the rest of the family feels when one member is destroying their financial security through a gambling addiction.

Extended unemployment can bring anger into a family. If you are already living beyond your means and then an unexpected illness or a layoff at work causes you to be unemployed, you are in a volatile situation. Husbands and wives start blaming one another for the mess they're in, but really, both have contributed to the crisis. They have probably both overspent and never saved anything, but when the flow of income is cut off, they get angry and want to blame someone.

Whenever the emphasis is on money and not on relationships, you will see stress, hurt, and anger running rampant. Relationships will be strained to the breaking point, and the joy that should be found with family and loved ones will be nonexistent. Life becomes hard and unfulfilling because the priorities are all out of line.

Your first line of defense to protect your family from an undue emphasis on money is to say, "Whatever happens to my finances is secondary to what goes on in my relationships. Money is not my god, and my family relationships mean more to me than gold or silver. I want truly extraordinary relationships in my family." With that as your priority, you will be well on the road to having the kind of relationships that you desire.

Restoring Financial Health

None of us have done everything right in our financial lives. We've all lost our focus from time to time and emphasized material goods more than we should have. If your desire, however, is to honor God and bless your family, He will help you in this important area of your life. First, make the commitment to put God and relationships before all pursuit of money and material possessions. Then, begin taking practical steps towards maximizing the stewardship of what God has placed in your hands.

Dr. Harry Jackson, Jr. has written an excellent book

called *In-laws, Outlaws, and the Functional Family* (Gospel Light Publications: Ventura, California, 2002) on family issues, including finances. Borrowing from some of his ideas using a medical motif, I'd like to share with you four specific steps you can take to restore financial health in your family.

Stop the bleeding!

Whenever a patient is brought into the emergency room of a hospital, those in attendance immediately check to see if the patient is bleeding. If there is a gaping wound with blood gushing out or a hemorrhage in the body, the patient will die unless the blood flow is stopped. It's the same way in your finances. If you are overspending and living beyond your means, the money is flowing out of you faster than you can replace it. You are bleeding to death, financially speaking, and unless you take immediate, decisive action, your finances are going to be wiped out.

The way you stop the bleeding in your finances is to set up and follow a budget. Now I know some of you don't like that word. To you, a budget means restriction, and you don't want that. You've been used to having the money come in one day and watching it go out the next. You never have enough to make it through the end of the month, but you prefer your "easy come, easy go" attitude to taking the steps necessary to change things.

A budget, when properly implemented, however, brings freedom, not restriction. It's the "fuel gauge" of your financial situation. In a car, the fuel gauge lets you know at any given time exactly how much gas you have. You can see at a glance if you have enough for a trip to the grocery store or if you'd better fill up before you go anywhere. When your fuel gauge is on empty, you don't get mad at it. You're glad to know where you stand, and you go and get some gas so that you will have the freedom to do what you want.

That's exactly what a budget can do for you. If you have

a written budget, you know precisely how much money you have available at any given time in the month. You know what bills you have paid and which ones are coming up. You know if you have enough money to buy a particular item or eat out or take a vacation. It's all written down for you in black and white.

A budget is really a plan for prosperity. A good budget helps you prioritize the spending of your money. As you learn to manage your money, you'll be able to get out of debt and even to start saving. If you haven't already done so, I urge you to set up a budget today and begin living by it. Once you develop the habit of responsible spending, you will begin to experience true financial freedom, and your relationships will be free of the unnecessary stress and tension that arise from overspending.

There are many, many excellent resources that are available to help you set up a realistic budget based on your income and monthly expenses. If you need help in this area, I would advise you to go to your local Christian bookstore and buy a good book that will help you get started. Of course, as a Christian, your tithe is the first thing to put in your budget: 10 percent right off the top of your income, before taxes. Then you lose a set amount to taxes, so that is not available to you. But from there, start listing your most important expenses, such as food, housing, and transportation. Be realistic, and don't fudge on the numbers to make it look like you have fewer expenses than you really do have. The budget needs to be truthful and realistic if it is going to help you. So list all your monthly expenses just as they are.

Many times after listing the expenses, you surprisingly discover that there should be money left over each month. You actually earn enough, but somehow you never seem to be quite able to make ends meet. In that case, there are probably some things you're doing that are draining you financially, even though you're not aware of it. Maybe you eat out for lunch every day, rather than bringing your lunch to work. Have you stopped to consider that if you eat out for lunch each weekday and spend just $5 a day, then in a year you will spend $1,300 on lunch? And if your husband or wife is doing the same, then between the two of you, you are spending $2,600 per year just on lunch! The list could go on and on as to how we waste money: buying coffee at the convenience store every morning, getting the kids a little toy every time we go into a store, never comparison shopping, etc. I'm not saying you should never do any of these things; I'm just saying you need to examine your spending and cut back on waste that you may not have been aware of.

The second way to stop the bleeding in your finances is to do a little "plastic surgery," if necessary. That means cut up your credit cards if you can't control your use of them. Most people spend a third more with credit cards than without them. It happens like this: Maybe you're going to the mall to buy a pair of diamond earrings that cost $400. Now that's a lot of money, but you've decided you really want those earrings, so you go to the jewelry store with $400 cash in your wallet. When you go into the store and start taking those hundred dollar bills out of your wallet—one by one you count out those Benjamins—you suddenly realize just how much money you are actually spending. As you start to hand that hard-earned cash to the clerk, you might just decide that you don't need those earrings after all. You've got twenty more pairs at home, and nobody's going to notice these new ones any more than they did the old ones. And even if they do notice you have new earrings, they'll probably just think they're made of zirconium! So what's the point?

But if you walk into the store with a credit card to purchase the same earrings, you don't have the same sense of cold hard cash leaving your pocket. You just walk into the store, set the card on the counter for the clerk to ring up the sale, and while he's busy with it, you drift over to another counter. Before you know it, you see a bracelet that matches perfectly with the earrings, and it's on sale, too, so you buy it. You make your way back over to the clerk and sign your name to the charge slip, spending more than you intended when you walked into the place.

Well, the end of the month arrives, and you get your credit card statement. You look at that bill and think, "There must be a mistake. I couldn't have spent that much money." But you did, and now you have to pay for it. That's why using credit cards is so dangerous. They give you an illusion of prosperity because you can buy whatever you want, but you forget that payback is right down the road.

Do whatever you have to in order to control credit card spending. I heard about one lady who took her credit card, put it in a jar of water, and then placed it in the freezer. Then if she went out and saw something she wanted to buy on credit, she'd have to go home, get the jar, defrost it, retrieve the credit card, and go back to the store to buy the item. Just knowing she had to go through all that rigmarole usually convinced her that she really didn't want the item that bad.

You know if you are weak in this area. If your credit cards control you rather than you control them, then it's time to get rid of them! If you do use credit cards, pay the balance each month, and never use them to buy items that you want but really can't afford.

Another thing that may cause you to spend too much is overexposure to television and other media sources. The more television commercials you watch, the more you're tempted to spend. You might be watching television, just relaxing, when all of a sudden a commercial comes on for a new, never-before-advertised special fishing lure. You watch, mesmerized, dreaming of all the fish you could catch with this latest, greatest gizmo. You dash for the phone to place your order before they're all gone. "What's the number?" you call to your wife. "1-800-flashing lure?" You call, place the order, and when the thing arrives, you promptly put it in your tackle box, where it sits for the next ten years.

It's the same way with catalogs. The more time you spend browsing through catalogs, the more things you're going to find that you want to buy. Advertisers know this; that's why you're bombarded with catalogs and junk mail every day. They know if they can just get you to look at their product, there's a good chance you'll buy it.

Similarly, the more times you go out shopping, the more you're going to spend. To some people, shopping is a hobby, but I would advise you not to go shopping unless you really have to. If you go out to shop just for the sake of shopping, rest assured, you'll find something you "need" and will spend more than you intended. So stay out of the stores unless you have a legitimate reason for being there in the first place.

That includes the grocery store. Don't go shopping for food when you are hungry, and don't bring your spouse or children with you if they tend to throw all kinds of extra things in the cart. Make a list and stick to it. Curb the impulse to buy whatever strikes your fancy. Compare prices among the various brands and stores. Purchase on sale, when possible, and in bulk, when feasible.

If you want to stop the bleeding in your finances, then you must establish a realistic budget. In other words, you've got to "act your wage"! That means taking a good look at your financial resources and developing a plan that enables you to live within those parameters. If you don't make much money, then don't spend a lot of money. If you can't pay the balance on your credit card each month, then get rid of it. The average American credit card has $5,000 debt on it, and if you are paying only the minimum on your card each month, then you are literally throwing away money as you pay interest of 18 percent or even higher. The credit card company takes the interest you're paying and invests it; in effect, you are simply making the credit card company rich. I can think of much better uses of my money than that. So your first step in restoring financial health is to stop the bleeding, at all costs!

Insert the IV!

In a hospital setting, an IV can nourish a patient and deliver necessary medications. It is often an essential part of getting him healthy and able to function on his own again. Sometimes getting the patient ready for the IV and actually starting it can be uncomfortable, but the patient endures it because he knows it's the only way to get the necessary nutrients and medicines into his body.

After you stop the bleeding in your finances, you are going to have to infuse new sources of cash into your system. It might be uncomfortable or even painful, but unless you get more cash flowing into your situation, you'll never improve in your financial health. You'll stay right where you are, weak and sick in financial matters and unable to get ahead.

There are a number of ways you can get more cash flowing into your life. To begin with, when you make up your budget and eliminate the sources of waste, take that amount and apply it toward debt reduction. That should be a top priority for you: to eliminate debt, especially credit card debt. You might want to consider temporarily taking a second job in order to whittle down your debt. Consider that option carefully. You don't want to never be home with your family, but you can't thrive as a family under a mountain of debt, either. If you take a second job, commit all of it to reducing your debt and view it as temporary.

Years ago I dealt with a man who was $100,000 in credit card debt. He had a good job, but he had managed to incur this tremendous amount of debt. Determined to get his financial house in order, he began a T-shirt business on the side, silk-screening T-shirts and then selling them. He actually developed a thriving business from the enterprise, and in two years he had paid off his $100,000 of debt. He found a new source of cash and infused it into his finances.

There's something you can do to help pay off your debts. You might have a hobby that you could turn into a resource for bringing in more cash. You might be good at yard work and could mow yards and do landscaping for others. You might be a stay-at-home mom who could care for children in your home. Maybe you're an excellent typist and can type term papers or legal documents at home. Whatever you can do, do it, and make sure to apply the extra cash to debt retirement.

Another way to increase your cash flow is by getting rid of excess stuff. You'd be surprised at how much stuff you have around your house that you could sell and make money from. Do you really need three cars when there are only two of you in the house? What about all those baby things you don't need anymore? You don't have to keep hanging on to the crib or the bassinet for sentimental reasons. Get rid of anything you're not using anymore. Sell the larger items, and apply that money to your debt. Then gather all the smaller items and have a garage sale. You'd be surprised how much you might make, and you can put that on your debt, too.

When you hold on to stuff that you don't need, it costs you money. You've got to house all your possessions, pay insurance on expensive items, and clean and maintain your things. It's also an emotional drain on you to live in a cluttered environment. It's hard to think straight when you are surrounded by stuff, stuff, and more stuff. But when you streamline and simplify your environment, it has a positive effect on how you think and can even bring some much-needed cash flowing into your situation.

Start rehab!

Once the patient in the hospital has stopped the bleeding and started the IV, it's time for him to begin his program of recovery. It's time for him to start taking the medicine, doing the therapy, and going to the rehab sessions that are going to help him get back on his feet again.

In your financial life, debt is the disease! It is the one thing that will ruin your financial health more than anything else. Much of the stress and pressure in life arises from unresolved debt. If you can get a handle on that and be willing to take the necessary "medicine" and undergo strenuous "rehab," you can get financially healthy again. It won't happen overnight, but gradually your financial stability will improve if you will be diligent at doing those things that aid in the return of financial health.

I've heard it said that in America, we ride on a bond-financed highway in a bank-financed car full of credit-card gas going to a savings-and-loan-financed home full of installment-plan furniture! How sadly true that is for most of us. But when you begin financial rehab, you can break out of that endless pattern of spending, charging, and living beyond your means.

Debt reduction is the rehab you're going to have to commit to if you want to regain your financial health. That might seem like a bitter pill to swallow, but once you get started and see the progress you're making, you'll welcome it in your life. Debt reduction simply means that you are going to come up with a specific plan for paying off your debts. You're not going to just continue spending and hope that one day somehow you'll get everything paid for. You're going to commit to a specific, methodical way to pay off your debts, taking the steps necessary to achieve that goal.

To get started, take a sheet of paper and draw a line down through the middle. On the left side of the paper, list all your debts from smallest to largest. On the right side of the paper, list your debts from those exacting the highest interest to those charging the least. Then begin paying off your debts from the top of the paper. In other words, as you get cash flowing into your situation, pay off the smallest debt first. Draw a red line through it when you have paid it. There's something about seeing that debt marked off that gives real encouragement and incentive to continue.

At the same time, start paying off the debts that charge the highest interest rates, because they are costing you more than those that charge less. These kinds of debts are the ones that are making you bleed the most, and you've got to have a systematic plan to pay them off. As you pay them, cross them off one by one, just like you're doing on the left side of the paper. Once you see a little progress being made, you gain momentum and are energized to work even harder towards achieving your goal of debt reduction.

If you'll follow this plan, eventually you will make your way down that sheet of paper and one day be totally out of debt. Living in debt is not God's way for you, and when you realize that and start doing what you have to in order to get out of debt, God will intervene on your behalf and help you. He wants to bless you, and He wants you to have all that you need, but He doesn't want you living in debt to make it happen.

Plan for full recovery!

Once you have a budget in place, increased cash flow, and a plan for debt reduction, you are well on your way to full financial health. There's just one thing that remains to complete your recovery, and that's to start saving. Some of you are wondering, "Pastor, should I save even while I am trying to pay off my debts?" To that I would answer, "Yes, you should," because saving is really a principle. It's not so much about the amount you are able to save as it is about the discipline and commitment to making this a principle in your life.

In the Bible, Joseph established the principle of saving, so I like to call this idea the "Joseph principle." When Joseph was put in charge of Pharaoh's palace, he immediately implemented the plan of saving because he knew that a famine was coming to the land. He stored one-fifth of the crops so that the people would have food during the time of need (Gen. 41:34, 40). Like Joseph, you have to have a plan of saving so that you will have a reserve during times of financial need. Sooner or later, you will hit a rough patch in your finances, and if you have built a reserve, it can carry you over until you get on your feet again.

I recommend that you take your income and set aside the first 10 percent for tithing. Take the next 10 percent and save it. Use the remaining 80 percent to live on. This is the principle that John D. Rockefeller attributed as the factor that enabled him to amass his fortune. That's how wealth and financial stability usually come: little by little as the result of seemingly small but consistent steps of wise financial management. Few people, unfortunately, believe this. They think that if they could just get lucky and win the lottery or if they could inherit a lot of money, then they would be set for life. They don't grasp the connection between what they do now with what they will have later.

Most people don't tithe or save, and they just live off everything they earn (and more, when you factor in credit card debt). In fact, most people are walking a dangerous tightrope of financial risk. If they were to lose their jobs or face a serious illness, they could make it only days, because their savings are so small. That might be somewhat understandable for non-Christians, but for those of us who profess faith in Christ, it should not be that way! We should have not only enough to meet our needs, but also extra stored away to carry us in times of crisis or to have available for blessing others.

Everyone should open a short-term savings account. Joseph constructed storehouses to hold the excess grain of Egypt, and when you open a savings account, you are establishing a storehouse for your financial resources. Even if you can't immediately allocate 10 percent of your income for savings, go ahead and open the account. Commit to the principle of saving and start small, if necessary. But be consistent and increase your percentage of savings as God blesses you. Have a goal of at least three months' expenses to be kept in your account. When you and your family know that something is tucked away for a rainy day, much financial stress and tension in the home dissolves. It is scriptural to save, not because we believe we can be our own source of security, but because we are being good stewards of what God has entrusted to us.

Once you have established short-term savings, begin considering investing as you are able. There are many knowledgeable people you can consult who can help you devise a plan of investment for the future. They can guide you toward safe investments, not some "get rich quick" scheme. Always be leery of those who promise you much for little. If it sounds too good to be true, then it probably is! But safe, practical investments continued for years can bring unbelievable returns.

Having the proper perspective on finances in your family is vital. Undue emphasis on money and possessions never brings fulfillment and close family ties. Examine your financial health. Do you have a budget? Do you have a steady flow of cash coming into your finances? Are you taking steps to eliminate debt? Have you begun a consistent plan of saving? If you can answer yes to these questions, then you are on the way to having true financial freedom. When your finances are in order and you are being a good steward of your resources, your relationships will flourish. You can move from ordinary, stale relationships where you're stressed out and never have enough to extraordinary relationships where you live in peace with God and others. That's my goal for my family, and I want it for yours, too!

CHAPTER 5

Extraordinary Communication: Speaking and Listening in Relationships

Everyone is in relationship with somebody. We all have families, friends, acquaintances, neighbors, and coworkers that we see on a regular basis. We can go through life largely ignoring these relationships and taking them for granted, or we can devote ourselves to building intimate relationships that nourish and enhance. If you want to have extraordinary relationships, then you're not going to be able to go merrily through life doing whatever you want and just expecting everything to fall into place. Extraordinary relationships result from extraordinary commitment and effort—they don't just happen. And key to having extraordinary relationships is learning how to communicate in a way that fosters the growth of intimacy.

The passage from Ecclesiastes 3 that we've been discussing has some relevant words to share concerning communication. Verse 7 says that there is "a time to keep silence, and a time to speak." In communicating, you can do one of two things with your tongue: you can use it, or you can subdue it! You can let it run wild, saying anything and everything, or you can learn to control it. Now most of us have no problem using the tongue; in fact, for some of us, that little tongue flaps constantly. It's the controlling of the tongue that's difficult. It's as though that small piece of flesh has a life all its own.

James 1:9 says, "But the tongue can no man tame; it is an unruly evil, full of deadly poison." All of us have such trouble controlling our tongues, especially when we get angry. At those times, it seems we just spew forth with the most deadly poison, saying things we don't mean and later regret. The tongue, though one of the smallest parts of our bodies, can do such damage, just like a tiny spark can set an entire forest on fire.

Spoken words, good or bad, possess tangibility in the spiritual world. There is an inherent power in them that many people don't recognize. When Joshua spoke a curse upon anyone who would try to rebuild Jericho (Josh. 6:26), that curse came to pass hundreds of years later, just as he had said. Similarly, when Jesus cursed the fig tree that had no fruit, it withered and died (Mark 11:14, 21).

People often repeat the old adage "Sticks and stones may break my bones, but words will never hurt me." There may be some truth in that saying when you're trying to teach a child to ignore teasing, but think about it for a minute. Sticks and stones break bones, but bones can mend and grow back together. Words wrongly spoken, however, can cut so deep and hurt so much that a gaping wound in the heart results. Words are powerful, for both good and evil.

James 1:19 says, "Let every man be swift to hear, slow to speak, slow to wrath." There's a sequence there: Being quick to listen and slow to speak prevents anger from flaring up. The converse is also true. When we're quick to speak and slow to listen, anger and hurt feelings abound. Unfortunately, the latter scenario is all too true for most of us. We are so quick to speak our minds, and we really don't like listening to anybody. We'd much rather be doing the talking than doing the listening.

The tongue is so unpredictable. Have you ever blurted something out and as soon as the words were out of your mouth, you knew you shouldn't have said them? But it was too late; the words were already spoken and you couldn't retrieve them. You were shocked at what you said and wondered where in the world those words came from. But Jesus told us, "Out of the abundance of the heart the mouth speaketh" (Matt. 12:34). In other words, the words you speak reveal what is truly in your heart. Your tongue is only giving voice to what is in your heart.

You cannot disavow what your tongue speaks. The words arise from your heart, and you will have to deal with the issues of your heart if you want to change the way you speak. In your own willpower, you will never be able to control your tongue. It's like a snake, coiled there and just waiting to strike out when the conditions are favorable. Then when someone says something you don't like or does something that irritates you, there it goes—that tongue shoots out of your mouth like a frog catching a fly! You're almost like a spectator and you think, "Who said that? Did those words come out of my mouth? I couldn't have said that!" But you did.

When you begin living according to the admonition to be quick to listen and slow to speak, you'll begin discerning the right time and place to speak, as well as being able to recognize those times when you need to keep silent. That's what Ecclesiastes 3:7 is telling us: There's a time to be silent and a time to speak. And you have to know when it is the right time for either!

Knowing the time to speak seems easy to us, because most of us love to hear the sound of our own voices. But speaking the right words at the right time is actually like possessing "apples of gold in settings of silver" (Prov. 25:11 NIV). This proverb stems from an interesting practice in which craftsmen shaped ornamental golden apples to be placed in a silver bowl in the king's palace. The beautiful, priceless decoration was the centerpiece for the king's table and was admired by all. That's the value of words correctly spoken. They are cherished and enhance relationships, adding to their value.

Anytime there is an overabundance of something, its value decreases. Gold, silver, and diamonds, for example, are precious because they are rare. Similarly, when you choose your words carefully and speak them meaningfully, their value increases; when you talk all the time, your words begin losing some of their value. Proverbs bears this out in verses 19–20 of the tenth chapter: "In the multitude of words there wanteth not sin: but he that refraineth his lips is wise. The tongue of the just is as choice silver."

If you control the flow of your words, you make them precious, not cheap and ordinary. You lessen the chance of saying something you don't mean or saying it in a way that offends someone. That's the problem with some people: They have no control over their tongues. The flow is constant; it never stops. And because they talk unceasingly, their families and friends no longer value their words and begin tuning them out. They have cheapened their words simply by having so many of them. So let your words be few so that when you do speak, people listen and value what you say.

The Art of Listening

When you speak, you want someone to listen. You're not interested in talking if there is no one there to hear what you are saying. There is a vast difference, however, between hearing what someone is saying and truly listening to him. Hearing involves the physical ear, but listening is a skill that can be learned and must be developed.

You have probably experienced this with someone in your family. Maybe you were talking to your husband and he was nodding his head as you spoke, but all of a sudden, you looked at him and could tell by the glazed look on his face that he was not really listening to you. The words were going in one ear and out the other. There was no real comprehension, just a receiving of words. If you're like most people, you probably got irritated and accusingly asked, "Are you listening to me?"

Listening involves concentration and focus. You cannot truly listen to someone and do three other tasks at the same time. If you need to talk to your child, you probably make him turn off the TV and sit down facing you. You don't want him to be distracted as you talk, because you want him to listen carefully to what you are going to say. If you try to follow him from room to room as he's munching on a snack and talking on the phone, he might physically hear your voice, but he won't be able to really listen to you.

In Leviticus 14:25, I found a verse that I think is particularly applicable to learning how to listen. This chapter is referring to the cleansing of lepers and others with contagious skin diseases, but in it I also see principles that can help us develop listening skills. The verse reads, "The priest shall take some of the blood of the trespass offering, and put it upon the tip of the right ear of him that is to be cleansed, and upon the thumb of his right hand, and upon the great toe of his right foot." Notice the three places where the blood was to be applied: the ear, the thumb, and the toe. Those three parts of the body can represent three areas in developing good listening skills.

Listening

In the Old Testament, a leper had to be separated from everyone else in society because he was unclean. In fact, lepers generally lived alone, apart from everyone else. Basically, leprosy meant separation and no communication with others. If the leper did venture out, he could go no closer to someone than 300 feet, and he had to cry, "Unclean! Unclean!" as he passed by. In applying this to communication, the leper can represent a person who has poor communication skills, a person who is emotionally separated from his family and friends because he doesn't know what to say or how to listen.

If, by some miracle, a leper was healed, he had to go to the high priest, who would then follow a specific procedure to pronounce the leper clean and fit for society. During this examination, the priest applied the blood of the sacrifice to three parts of the leper's body. The first place to which blood was applied was the ear. This is where listening begins. A person speaks, and the words are received within the physical organ of the ear. You can receive those audible sensations of sound within your ear and hear in the physical sense of the word, but that doesn't mean that you have listened.

A few years back, I discovered that I needed work in this area. My wife and I would be talking, and I thought I was listening to what she was saying. But then I would make a statement to add something to the conversation, and she would respond, "I already said that."

I would answer, "No, you didn't say that. I don't remember you saying anything like that."

And she would say, "Well, I did say it; you just weren't listening." And she was right! I realized that sometimes when she was talking, I was thinking about something else. As a result, I heard the words but missed the message. I thought the problem was with her, but really it was with me.

It's like the joke a friend of mine told me: A man thought his wife was going deaf, so he consulted an audiologist as to what to do about it. He wanted to know an easy way he could check her hearing at home. The audiologist said, "Well, all you need to do is stand about 20 feet behind her, call her name, and ask her a question. If she doesn't respond, move closer and repeat the question. Do this until she answers you, and then you'll know how bad the hearing loss is."

The man went home and walked into the kitchen where his wife was preparing dinner, stirring a pot on the stove. He was about 20 feet away, and he said, "Sweetheart, what's for dinner?" No response. "This is terrible," he thought, so he moved a little closer and repeated the question: "Sweetheart, what's for dinner?" Still no response. She just stood there, stirring her pot, and the man thought, "This is worse than I imagined." He repeated the process two more times, until finally he was only 2 feet behind her. "Sweetheart, what's for dinner?" he asked once more.

His wife turned around and looked at him and said, "For the fourth time, I said 'spaghetti'!" He thought she had the problem, but all along, he was the one who couldn't hear. Sometimes we blame others for poor communication, but we are the ones who don't know how to listen.

Your mind can easily tune out what you're not interested in. If you want to truly listen—not just hear—you are going to have to make a concerted effort to that end. Put down whatever you are doing, turn in the direction of the one speaking, and look at the eyes and mouth as the person speaks. Listen to what is being said, and reconstruct in your mind what you are being told. Don't just sit there nodding your head, but all the while planning what you are going to say as soon as you can get a word in edgewise. That is not listening! True listening moves past simply hearing the words uttered.

Grasping

The second place to which the high priest applied the blood was the thumb. The thumb is the instrument by which you grasp something, and in communication, you have to move past just listening to the words to learning how to grasp their true meaning and intent. In other words, you have to understand what is being said.

Understanding encompasses much more than hearing the words and listening to them. True understanding comes from reading between the lines. It's not just what your child or spouse says, but how he says it that will clue you in to understanding what is going on. For example, if you walk through the living room and one of your children is just sitting there sniffling, you'll probably say, "What's wrong?" Many times the child will give the rote answer: "Nothing."

If you walk away and say, "Okay, I'm glad you're fine," you've missed it, big time! You heard what the child said, but you also noticed he was crying. Something is obviously wrong, even if he doesn't express it verbally. Right at this critical juncture is where a lot of us miss it. We hear the words, but miss the message.

If you are going to have extraordinary communication in your relationships, learning to understand and grasp the message behind the words is crucial. When you are talking to someone, observe his body language, facial expressions, and emotions. These are all clues to what the person really means or feels about the issue. A good practice to develop is to speak back to the person what you are hearing to make sure that you understand what is being said.

Acting

The third place where the blood was applied to the leper was on his big toe. The big toe, as part of the foot, represents action. Our feet give us mobility and enable us to go places. Without the feet, we would have no ability to put into action anything that required movement. After we have listened to what someone is saying and have understood the message conveyed, we still have to act in a relevant fashion. When we respond appropriately to something that was spoken, the person then knows that we have truly heard him.

The Lord told the prophet Ezekiel that even though the people were listening to him, they weren't implementing appropriate action. Ezekiel 33:31 NIV reads, "My people come to you, as they usually do, and sit before you to listen to your words, but they do not put them into practice." They heard the words, but they didn't do anything about it. They were, like James says, "hearers of the word," but not "doers" (James 1:22). That type of behavior doesn't please the Lord and will never help you learn how to communicate in an extraordinary fashion.

All too often, couples have a discussion about something and both parties promise they are going to do better. They say they are going to change some behavior that is not helping the marriage, but then they fail to follow through. If that happens too many times, trust suffers, and hope for intimacy fades. So, you see, it is imperative that you not only listen to your spouse and understand what is being said, but also that you follow through with appropriate action.

Sometimes I like to sharpen my younger sons' listening abilities. I'll be sitting in the kitchen and will tell one of them, "Go into my bathroom and get my green checkbook. Bring it to me here in the kitchen." He disappears and comes back in just a little while, carrying a book I've been reading. I'll question him, "What's that you've got?"

He answers, "Well, you told me to go get your book. Here it is."

"No, not the book, but my checkbook is what I said," I'll reply. He goes out of the room again and comes back with a checkbook, but not the green one I asked for. We continue this process until he gets it right. I do this because I want my son to learn how to focus on what I am saying, to understand accurately the request, and then to initiate the proper action necessary to fulfill the request. It is so vital that all of us learn those three aspects of communication: listening, grasping, and acting. Mastering those skills is essential for any family that wants to have extraordinary communication.

The Art of Speaking

Just as you have to develop listening skills, so, too, do you have to develop the art of speaking. There is a time and a place, as well as a right way, to say something, and if you'll learn that, you'll be more likely to have healthy communication in your relationships. If you ignore that fact and think you can blab anything you want any old time you want, you'll find your relationships suffering.

Any discussion of communication must first address the fact that the sexes are inherently different in the way they communicate. The brains of men and women are actually wired differently, and the way they perceive things and express thoughts is very different, too.

The brain has two main sides: the left side and the right side. The left side of the brain is the logical, problem-solving part, while the right side is the emotional, creative side. When a child is forming in its mother's womb, something unique happens in the baby's development, if it is a female. At a given time in a baby girl's development, there is a shower of hormones that causes the two lobes of her brain to connect in such a way that a great deal of communication can occur between the two sides. This enables females to use both portions of their brains in an interrelated fashion much more than males can. Males do have and use both lobes of the brain, but they tend to be dominated by the left side of the brain and don't have as much communication between the two parts.

For that reason, a man may take a while to demonstrate emotion in a situation where his wife is already experiencing deep feelings. He processes the information in an analytical, logical way, and it takes a little while to travel over to the right side where his emotions lie. His wife, however, has no difficulty switching between reason and emotion—and sometimes she does so very quickly! A man who doesn't understand this basic difference between the sexes will not be a skilled communicator with his wife.

Generally speaking, men are quick to speak and offer a solution when their wives, children, or others present a problem. They feel most comfortable giving a quick-fix, blanket answer that they think solves the problem. This is particularly irritating for their wives because women often like to verbalize a problem and want their husbands to listen to them and understand. They are not so much interested in the solution as they are in feeling that their husbands care about them and understand what they are trying to say.

Women are often able to solve their problems simply by talking them through. Many husbands fail to realize this, however, and the moment their wives begin talking, they interrupt with a logical solution to the problem. For example, maybe little Timmy is failing math. The woman tells her husband after dinner one evening, "Honey, we got a note today saying that Timmy is failing math. I wonder if it's because I'm not home as much since I took that part-time job . . ."

Her husband hears only the first statement and interrupts, "Well, we can fix that. No television and straight to his room for homework when Timmy gets in from school. That'll bring his grade up. Now, anything else I can help with?"

This man thinks he has solved the problem, because all he heard was that Timmy was failing math. Quite pleased with himself, he presents an easy solution to the problem and is ready to tackle the next one. But he failed to grasp his wife's fears and concerns about working and how that affected Timmy. What his wife really needed was for her husband to listen to her voice her concerns and then take her in his arms and tell her what a great mother she was. He needed to let her talk it out, and with her come up with a viable plan to help little Timmy.

When a husband fails to understand what his wife needs, she feels like she is alone in the problem. It is very frustrating for her to have her husband immediately jump in with a solution when she is troubled about something. She may become so upset with the situation that she bursts into tears! Most men get very uncomfortable with a crying woman. The more she cries, the more he wants to "fix it."

"Now, Darling . . . Sweetheart . . . there's no need to cry. I know what to do." She cries harder.

"There's no reason to get upset; it's no big deal." The tears are coming like a river now.

"Now, look here. You need to just turn off the faucet. You're overreacting." She runs from the room, crying her heart out.

The bewildered husband has no idea where he missed it. All he was doing was trying to make his wife see there was nothing to worry about. But the more he tried to fix it, the more she cried! What he failed to understand was the fact that a distressed woman would rather be held than lectured. So, husbands, remember that the next time your wife is upset about something.

I have found another thing that husbands need to do concerning communication is to provide direction and verbalize decisions that affect the family. I don't know why it is, but many men have a very difficult time making decisions. They are content to mull the issue over in their minds, chew on it like a cow does with its cud, swallow it down, let it come up again in a few days, chew on it some more, and one day down the road make a decision. When the decision is finally made, the husband blurts it out one day and the wife is caught totally off guard. She wasn't aware of what he was thinking, and she doesn't like to have things suddenly thrust upon her. She wants to know what the husband is considering and when he is going to make a decision. She likes for there to be plenty of time between the decision reached and the decision implemented.

When a husband and wife have a decision to make, it's good for both of them to first acknowledge that a decision needs to be made. That's the basic starting point, because to the husband, it might not be all that important to reach a decision, but to his wife, it's critical to know what they are going to do. I recommend that when a decision needs to be reached, both husband and wife agree upon a set time by which the decision will be made. Then the wife should back off and let her husband process the information. During that time, she can't keep bugging him for a decision; she's got to leave him alone. But when the day comes that they agreed upon to reach a decision, the husband can procrastinate no longer. He must sit down with his wife, discuss the issue with her, and conclude the matter. This technique gives the husband time to think without pressure but doesn't leave the wife hanging indefinitely.

Besides the gender differences in communications, there are many other things to consider in moving communication to an extraordinary level. These are "apples of gold" that both men and women can use. Let's discuss three of these.

Pictures and parables

Jesus is the example for everything in our lives, and that includes communication. If you study the New Testament, you find that Jesus often used parables and stories to communicate truths and lessons to His followers. You are familiar with many of them: the prodigal son, the tares and the wheat, the sower and the seed, the widow and the unjust judge, and many others. Jesus knew how to communicate in such a way that it created a picture in the mind of the one listening, and that's a valuable skill to learn.

Even in the Old Testament, we see many examples of

the prophets speaking in parables or symbolic language to impart a revelation. For some reason, we seem better able to grasp an idea or a feeling when it is expressed in a pictorial or storytelling form. Take the story of the prophet Nathan and David, for example. David sinned grievously by committing adultery with Bathsheba and then having her husband, Uriah, killed in an attempt to cover up the sin. To all outward appearances, it looked like David had gotten away with it. One day, however, Nathan shows up at David's house. He says, "David, I want to tell you a little story." He proceeds to tell him the story of a man who owned one little lamb and another man who owned an abundance of sheep and cattle. The rich man had a visitor, and instead of taking an animal from his flock to serve as food, he took the other man's lamb, killed it, and served it to his guest.

David, listening to the story, becomes enraged and vehemently declares, "That guy deserves to die! How could anyone do such a thing!" At this point, he fails to recognize himself in the story and self-righteously pronounces judgment.

Nathan boldly asserts, "David, you are that man!" and he reveals David's hidden sin (2 Sam. 12:1–7). Only then are David's eyes opened, and he is forced to confront the gravity of his sin. The story that Nathan told hit with such force that David could no longer think he had hidden his sin and gotten away with it.

That's the impact of a parable or timely example. If Nathan had gone to David with both guns blazing, accusing him of his sin and saying, "I know what you did; you're a murderer, David; you're nothing but an adulterer. God is going to judge you for it," he would have been correct in everything he said, but David's response may have been totally different. When people are directly attacked or confronted, they will often react defensively, but when a neutral example is presented, it enables them to see the truth of the situation in an unthreatening way.

So if you're having a hard time communicating something, stop for a minute and see if you can recall a story from the Bible or an incident in real life that will help you to present your thoughts. Then use the story to explain how you are feeling. Many times that will enable the other person to understand you better and empathize with your feelings.

Time and place

There is a right time and a right place for communicating on a deeper level. If you and your spouse are having a disagreement about something, you cannot solve it on the run. Don't bring up the issue as you're walking out the door for work. There is no time to work the problem out, and you'll probably just make it worse by "stirring the pot" when you don't have time to finish.

If it's a small problem or minor irritation, it can possibly be dealt with on the spot, but if it is a problem that's ongoing and reflective of deeper issues, you're going to have to select a definite time and place for a discussion of it. Lengthy, deep subjects need special, designated time. It may require hours to discuss it and work it through. But first, decide on the time when you are going to discuss the issue.

Next, select the place for the discussion. Not any old place will do! You've got to have a setting that is conducive for communication. You can't have the children running around, the phone ringing, the television blaring, and the doorbell ringing and think that you are going to get anywhere in solving the problem. So take care of the kids first. Send them off to visit Grandma if you need to, or schedule the discussion after their bedtime, but make sure they are not going to be interrupting you.

During the discussion, turn off all the phones and set aside every other activity. Don't be jumping up to check the soup on the stove or to go feed the dog. All those other things can wait. This time is designated solely for discussing the problem and talking it out to an acceptable conclusion. Stick with the issue at hand, and don't get distracted.

Levels of communication

Communication exists on various levels, and each level has its place. The lowest level of communication is the casual level: "How was your day?" "What's for dinner?" "Hasn't the weather been gorgeous?" That level is fine for ordinary talking, but it can't be the extent of your communication if you want real closeness and intimacy. You need to move up a level!

At the second level, the contemplative level, you're thinking a little bit more and starting to share your feelings to some degree. On this level, you might actually describe your day at the office, share the new recipe you're using for dinner, or discuss the weather trends that are giving you the beautiful weather. This is all good, and most of the time you might stay right here in your communication, but there is yet a third level.

The third level is the confrontational level. Now you are offering deeper thoughts and opinions. You're sharing how you felt when the boss reprimanded you, or the disappointment you experienced when the new recipe flopped. You are expressing how you truly feel about some issue.

Some people feel threatened at this level. They don't feel free to express an unpopular opinion or a negative emotion. They don't say anything that's too revealing, and although everything seems fine on the surface, they are missing out on forming extraordinary relationships. Ordinary relationships stay at the first and second levels, but only the third level will get you to a stage where you are free to express true feelings.

When you are having a discussion of an important issue and you have set aside a time and place for it, move through the three levels of communication. Don't go into the situation and immediately try to jump to the confrontational level. That would be like a plane taking off and trying to immediately reach cruising altitude. The plane ascends gradually, getting clearance at each level of flight.

Maybe your child is not doing well in school. Don't call him into his bedroom and immediately light in to him, demanding to know what's going on and why, and then doling out the punishment. Try walking into his room, sitting down on the edge of the bed with him, and initiating the conversation. Start at the bottom: "How's school going?" Give him time to talk on that level for a little bit. Then you move up a bit: "How are you doing in science class? Do you understand everything? Doing your homework? Do you need help?" Again, let the child talk, encouraging him to express how he feels about science class. Finally, proceed to the more serious, confrontational level: "I got a call from your teacher. She says you're failing science. Why do you think that is?"

As you move slowly from level to level, you give the child a chance to express himself, and you have the opportunity to gain insight into his true feelings. By the time you come to the thornier aspect of the issue—why is he failing?—the child has had time to talk some of it out. He's likely to be much more open to any correction, plus by gradually raising the confrontational level of the conversation, you keep the problem from escalating out of control.

At any level of communication, your choice of words is critical. According to Proverbs 18:21, "Death and life are in the power of the tongue: and they that love it shall eat the fruit thereof," and a wise person knows that. Speech is a gift from God to human beings; no other creature can articulate words into a discernible language with syntax and structure. Only people can do that.

Although God is the giver of speech and language, you are the one who chooses the particular words you say. You can speak death, or you can speak life—the choice is yours. That is a sobering thought when you stop to think about it. Every relationship in your life is being either built or destroyed by the words you freely choose. The words you choose bring fruit, both good and bad, and you are eating of the fruit of your words.

Luke 6:45 says, "A good man out of the good treasure of his heart bringeth forth that which is good; and an evil man out of the evil treasure of his heart bringeth forth that which is evil: for of the abundance of the heart his mouth speaketh." Your words originate from within your heart; they are merely a reflection of your inner beliefs and attitudes. Furthermore, once you speak a word, you can't take it back. You can't just say, "Oh, I didn't mean it" and expect a person to forget something hurtful you said. The words you spoke are emblazoned on his brain; he has recorded it in his memory, just like a tape recorder captures words.

Once words are recorded on tape, you cannot deny you spoke them. Your own words can be replayed and replayed, convicting you over and over. That's why you've got to be so careful about what you say. You can't afford to run your mouth and say whatever pops into your head in the heat of an argument. You'll destroy your relationships that way. If you say hurtful things and then try to retract them, you'll soon find that the damage has already been done, and only time and the Holy Spirit can heal the wound that you caused.

Paul admonishes us in Ephesians 4:29 to speak only those things that are good and helpful and that will build others up. If you obeyed that one verse, it would prevent you from saying things that you later regret. Words are a serious matter. Never forget their power, and never forget their ability to either build or destroy.

When you use words to bless and praise your spouse and children, you release a power in their lives that is greater than you realize. Women need to hear words of praise to establish their self-worth. When their husbands and children rise up and call them blessed (Prov. 31:28), a deep feeling of satisfaction and security envelopes them. When no one notices all their hard work and sacrifice, they feel deflated, like a balloon that's lost its air.

Children and men also need praise and affirmation. A child's confidence in his ability to cope in the world is strengthened when he has parents who praise him sincerely, who tell him how capable he is, and who express what a fine person of character he is becoming. Men need praise from their wives and others to establish a sense of security and to receive assurance that they are not foolish or inferior.

Some people have the wrong idea about praise. They say, "Well, I don't believe in all that praise talk. You're just going to give somebody a big head by saying all that stuff." They have missed the point: We all need to hear sincere words of affirmation if we are to be healthy, secure people in meaningful relationships. I know of so many men who as boys never got that word of affirmation they needed. They grew up just wanting to hear their dads say, "Atta boy. You're doing a great job." But they never got that, and they grew up with a void in their hearts and an inability to affirm others.

Years ago when I was in college, I had a friend who fell in love with a very attractive girl. This young lady was thin and looked like a model, but she had always thought of herself as skinny and unattractive. She had grown up in a family with four brothers, and her brothers were always teasing her, telling her how ugly and skinny she was. They probably meant no harm, but she recorded those words in her mind and believed them. As a result, she had no confidence in herself.

When my friend started dating the girl, she was very shy and reserved. Eventually they married, and years later I was in a meeting with this man. We began talking, and he told me to look across the room to where his wife was. This formerly shy, introspective young woman was now the picture of confidence and beauty. She flitted around the room like a beautiful butterfly. My friend looked at me and said—not in a boastful way, but in a truthful way—"That's what I've done with my words." He had recognized the true beauty and worth of this woman and had begun speaking affirming words to her. He told her how beautiful she was, how intelligent she was—things like that. His consistent use of sincere, loving praise had totally transformed his wife.

We all have that potential in our relationships. Your children and spouse are actually the sum total of what you've said about them and spoken to them. You've either built them up and caused their lives to prosper, or you've destroyed their confidence and brought them much suffering. You hold the key to determining the quality of your relationship with them.

No one can bless you and no one can wound you as much as someone you are close to. All of us have been hurt by words, and all of us have hurt others by our choice of words. When I am tempted to nurse a grudge against someone who has verbally hurt me, I think of Jesus dying on the cross. He felt the sting of all His friends turning their backs on Him and denying Him. He had to endure the cruel taunts and insults of the crowd and the rulers of His time. Even the thieves crucified with Him jeered and mocked Him. He, above all others, knew the hurt of spoken words. Yet He forgave.

If you will take to the cross every spiteful word that you've spoken and every hurtful word that was directed at you, you can have the opportunity to start over. You can receive forgiveness and extend forgiveness. You can retract through the power of the cross every wrong word you've spoken against someone. The blood of Jesus is that powerful. It can make all things new and truly usher in extraordinary relationships in your life.

CHAPTER 6

Extraordinary Harmony: Resolving Conflict in Relationships

All relationships, even extraordinary ones, will face conflict. People are different, and their views on things are not the same. Those who have extraordinary relationships have problems just like everyone else, but they have learned how to face their problems head on and resolve them. That is so critical in relationships. You can't keep sweeping problems under the rug and expect them to resolve on their own. If you don't take control of the problems, the problems will control you. Your relationships will suffer and the closeness you desire will never materialize.

There is a right way to handle conflict, and there is a wrong way. Unless you make a conscious decision to learn scriptural, godly ways of resolving your problems, you will probably do whatever your flesh dictates—and that is never good! Your natural tendency when facing a problem is to blame others and to get defensive when questioned concerning your part in it. You want others to change, not you!

God intends for your relationships, however, to refine

both you and those you're in relationship with. Proverbs 27:17 NIV says, "As iron sharpens iron, so one man sharpens another." When iron sharpens iron, there is contact and friction between the two surfaces. Sparks fly as a result, and when you are in relationship with others, sparks will fly, too! It's inevitable; you grate upon them and they grate upon you, and conflict erupts. This is not necessarily bad; it all depends upon how you view the conflict and how you resolve it.

When the sparks begin flying in a relationship, most people get heated and upset. They get very uncomfortable and just want the problem to go away. They feel threatened and hurt and wonder what went wrong in the relationship.

You may have thought like that. Maybe you assumed that if you were in a good relationship, then you would never have an argument or disagreement and would float merrily along through life. Nothing could be further from the truth!

In reality, relationships exist in God's plan as a way to develop character. God sends people into your life to rub across the grain, like a file sharpening a blade. These people may irritate you and not think like you, but God intends on using them to smooth out your rough edges. In other words, because you, like everyone else, have character flaws, God is going to bring people into your life to challenge you in those areas. He knows exactly who you need to have around to force you to face yourself and your flaws. If you tend to be impatient, He may surround you with people who try your patience. If you are overly regimented, He may surround you with very disorganized, impulsive people. Whatever your flaw, He wants to refine it and smooth it out in your life. He wants to sharpen your character and restore your cutting edge.

Once you acknowledge that relationships are meant to sharpen you, it makes it much easier to stop resenting conflict and start receiving the correction you need from it. You begin recognizing God's hand at work to hone you to a fine edge, and you begin cooperating with Him instead of trying to run from every conflict. There is, however, a progression in the process. Whenever God is developing your character, there will always come a conflict; this conflict then leads to crisis; and the crisis, ideally, leads to covenant. God's highest goal is for you to have covenant relationships, but you can never arrive at that point unless you first go through conflict and crisis.

Character Results from Conflict

Let's examine these three stages of moving from character development to conflict to covenant and see how God uses them to deepen our relationships and bring us from ordinary to extraordinary relationships. The story of Jacob and Laban as recorded in Genesis 31 provides our backdrop for understanding the process. In the earlier chapters of Genesis, Jacob had fled home after deceiving his brother, Esau, and had gone to his Uncle Laban's. For twenty years he had lived there, working the first seven years to earn the right to marry Laban's daughter Rachel. On the wedding day, however, Laban deceived Jacob, substituting his daughter Leah for Rachel. So Jacob worked seven more years to get the girl he was supposed to have in the first place. After marrying Rachel, Jacob stayed and worked for his uncle another six years.

For all those twenty years, Laban treated Jacob unfairly, manipulating and deceiving at every turn. Regardless of what Laban did to Jacob, Jacob prospered because God was watching out for him and taking care of him. Laban and his sons resented Jacob's prosperity and accused him of taking what was theirs. Jacob noticed their attitude towards him, and one day God directed him to return to the land of his fathers.

I can imagine that Jacob was delighted to hear that instruction from the Lord! He was finally going to be free of Laban. The relationship was going to be over, and he could return to his homeland. Perhaps to avoid conflict, Jacob gathered his wives, children, and flocks and left without saying anything to Laban. Three days after their departure, Laban discovered that they had departed, and he set off in hot pursuit. Before Laban tracked him down, however, God gave him a dream and told him to be careful of how he dealt with Jacob.

That dream was the only thing restraining Laban from killing Jacob. They had lived in tension for twenty years, and the sparks were flying now! He wanted to deal with Jacob once and for all and let him have it, but God protected Jacob and watched over him, just like He had always done before. So finally, in verse 26 Laban confronts Jacob and demands to know why he left in secret, taking Laban's daughters and grandchildren with him. A conflict between the two men had definitely erupted.

Before Jacob had gone to live in his uncle's land, he had been a deceiver and manipulator in his own family, usurping his brother's place. In fact, Jacob's very name meant "trickster," and that's what he had been all his life. Isn't it interesting that God led Jacob to a place where he would be confronted with a man who surpassed him in deception and manipulation? Jacob's character flaw caused God to put him in contact with someone who was just like him, only worse! The two men constantly butted heads because they were so much alike. But all that time, God was working on Jacob's character, chipping away at that deceptive nature little by little.

The very things you cannot tolerate in someone else are often reflections of your own flaws. Maybe you have a child who is chronically slow at everything you ask him to do. It irritates you to no end, until one day God shows you that you are late everywhere you go and constantly procrastinate. You saw the flaw in your child but didn't recognize it in yourself until God revealed it to you. God has a way of bringing people into your life who possess some of the same weaknesses you have or are so different from you that you cannot begin to understand what makes them tick. Either way, God is after your character. He wants to mold it and shape it and cause you to become more like Him. That's the purpose of relationships.

Your character flaws will unquestionably lead to conflict. God allows conflict so that you will be confronted with your true self and have the opportunity to change. If there were never any conflict, you might never come to the realization that you had things in your life that needed to change. You would probably just go through life following the path of least resistance. But when a conflict arises, you have to do something. You arrive at a moment of crisis.

Conflict Leads to Crisis

Jacob's character flaw led to his conflict with Laban. When he just couldn't take it anymore, he fled in the night, knowing he would anger Laban. But he was determined to leave; he had taken all he was going to take. He had drawn a line in the sand and said "No more!" The conflict had now become a full-blown crisis.

Whenever you have a conflict with someone and you don't resolve it as a small thing, it will eventually lead to a crisis. It might be twenty years down the road, like it was with Jacob, but unresolved conflict can lie dormant only so long. One day it will blow up in your face if you don't take care of it when it is a smaller problem. That's why you hear of men or women who have been married twenty-five years who suddenly announce to their spouses, "I'm leaving. I want a divorce. I'm not happy in this marriage and haven't been in years." They never learned how to deal with conflict and resolve it, and thus it built to a crisis level.

When the crisis between Jacob and Laban erupted, the only thing that kept Laban from killing Jacob was supernatural intervention. God appeared to Laban in a dream and warned him to be very careful of how he spoke to Jacob. So when Laban caught up with Jacob, he wanted explanations, but he restrained himself from doing harm. Because of that godly restraint that he accepted, the crisis was able to be resolved.

Crisis Leads to Covenant

Jacob and Laban were at meltdown. They were squared off, facing each other across the fence. Twenty years of deception, manipulation, betrayal, and jockeying for position had suddenly been thrust to the forefront. There would be no more ignoring the problem or hoping it would go away. The pot was boiling over, and the crisis was going to have to be dealt with now!

In verses 26–30 of Genesis 31, Laban lays out his case against Jacob, and in verses 36–42, Jacob presents his side of the picture. But by the time we get to verse 44, a beautiful testament of the healing power of covenant resolution emerges. Laban is speaking and says, "Now therefore come thou, let us make a covenant, I and thou; and let it be for a witness between me and thee." Or as the NLT version phrases it: "Come now, and we will make a peace treaty, you and I, and we will live by its terms."

Jacob responds in verses 45–46: "And Jacob took a stone, and set it up for a pillar. And Jacob said unto his brethren, 'Gather stones'; and they took stones, and made an heap: and they did eat there upon the heap." What an absolutely beautiful picture of reconciliation! Laban and Jacob, enemies for twenty years, sat down together in covenant fellowship.

Notice how Jacob took a stone and told those with him to gather stones. That is a significant action, because stones in his time were used to render judgment. If someone committed a grievous sin punishable by death, he was stoned. His own people would gather up stones and cast them at him until he died. But in this passage of Genesis, Jacob and his family took stones and used them to build an altar of reconciliation. And after that altar was built, they sat down together with Laban and shared a meal. Who would have ever thought that Laban and Jacob would sit down in peace and fellowship together? There was so much "water under the bridge" that it didn't seem possible that they could ever be reconciled. But, nevertheless, there they were—doing just that!

Can you imagine that happening in your family? Maybe you have a family member that you've been estranged from for years. You might not even remember what the original conflict was about; all you know is that you haven't spoken to each other in years. If that's the case, you face a choice. Will you continue to pick up the stones of offense and cast them? Or will you lay down those stones and build an altar with them? If God could restore Laban and Jacob, He can restore your family, too. But you've got to lay down the stones.

Ecclesiastes 3:5 says that there is "a time to cast away stones, and a time to gather stones together." It echoes what happened in the story of Jacob and Laban and what can happen in your family, too. You've got to be big enough to admit your mistakes, learn your character lesson, and let God use the crisis to mature you. It's time to lay down every stone, and instead use all those areas of conflict as stones to build your altar of covenant relationship.

Sources of Conflict

There are three main sources of conflict that you are going to experience in your relationships. Regardless of the source, however, the purpose of the conflict in God's eyes is to sharpen your character and lead you into covenant relationship. Understanding this will enable you to look at conflicts in a whole new way—not so much as a threat, but as an opportunity to deepen relationships.

Expectations

All relationships create expectations, consciously or unconsciously. When Jacob went to live with Laban and worked for him for seven years, he expected to be given his beloved Rachel in marriage. As you know, he was given Leah instead, and that was the beginning of twenty years of false promises and expectations in the relationship between uncle and nephew.

Poor communication will always lead to false expectations. False expectations lead to broken promises, and broken promises lead to rifts in relationships. It is so important to guard what you say so that what you convey with your words is what you truly mean. Sometimes someone can construe your words to be a promise to do something. To that person, what you said was binding and certain, but you actually had no intent of communicating that. You tell a child that you and he will go to the zoo soon, and he thinks you've promised to take him Saturday. So watch what you say and how you say it. Communication must be clear, direct, and to the point. Evasive, vague answers to questions will only lead to wrong assumptions and misunderstandings.

When most people marry, they bring a whole set of expectations with them, some of them very unrealistic. The wife sees her husband as the knight in shining armor who is going to take care of all her needs and provide for her. She assumes he'll fix the leaks in the roof and keep the oil changed in her car. She trusts that he will be such a good provider that she'll never have to work outside the home. Their house will be beautiful, and her knight, of course, will never speak a harsh word to her. On top of all that, she fully expects that they will have Bible study together each evening, and he will be the spiritual priest of their home. She has it all planned out!

At the same time, the husband has his own set of expectations. He expects his wife to be the Proverbs 31 woman of modern times. She will arise early and fix a full-course breakfast for him every day. She will never get behind on the laundry, and she will take care of disciplining the children. She will be smart, thrifty, and well-groomed at all times. She will excel in everything she does, and of course, she will never gain a pound!

On the wedding day, both partners are so starry-eyed that they actually believe their fantasies of marital bliss. But when the honeymoon is over and everyday life sets in, they soon find their life is not living up to their expectations. The roof leaks and the husband takes a month to repair it. The full-course breakfast turns out to be a bowl of soggy cornflakes. The "knight" spends every evening in front of the TV, and the "fair damsel" has no idea how to run a household. Both partners are disappointed with the way their marriage has turned out.

Sloppy, loose, ill-defined relationships are headed for trouble. When you expect certain things from others and they don't live up to your expectations, you get hurt and disappointed in them. You tend to withdraw just a little because you don't want to get hurt again. Over time, you pull back more and more until there's a huge wall between you and them.

Expectations must be clearly and verbally expressed, and agreed upon. Husbands and wives must know their roles as stated in Ephesians 5 and discuss what that means in daily living. I know that as husband I'm supposed to be the head of my family, which means I'm my wife's guardian and protector. I know that she and my children look to me for spiritual leadership, so I do my best to provide that, too. In turn, Melanie knows her role. She is my helpmate, equal with me in the things of God. She loves and serves me, just as I do her. When we have a decision to make, we discuss the issue together, and I value her input. We will try our best to arrive at a mutually acceptable decision, but if that is not possible, she will defer to me.

By both of us understanding and accepting our roles within the family, as well as the children also doing so, we are able to avoid much unnecessary conflict. But without those clearly defined roles that shape our expectations, we would be cruising towards constant conflict.

Arguments

A second source of conflict is arguments. One guy said, "My wife and I don't ever argue; we just have animated discussions"! You can call it whatever you want, but you know what an argument is. Sharp, cross words are uttered in an argument, and a heated exchange often takes place.

Generally speaking, there are two types of arguments. The first kind arises simply because you are tired, hungry, overworked, or even bored! A situation comes up that you don't like and you snap at someone. He snaps back, and before you know it, you are arguing over something that's not worth the time it takes to talk about it. I'm talking about things like "Why don't you ever put the top back on the toothpaste?" or "How could you forget to pick up the dry cleaning?" These kinds of arguments are really meaningless, and unless you allow them to escalate to a higher level, they will often resolve on their own. Sometimes it only takes a little sleep, a little rest, or a bite to eat to make you feel better. That's because the argument is petty and of no account.

But the second, more serious type of argument deals with expectations and roles. This type of argument is not so easily resolved, and a little sleep or food is not going to fix anything. That's because the argument deals with deeper issues that may have been a source of trouble for a long time.

The first kind of argument is like having a bruise. It hurts a little bit but soon goes away without any special treatment. An argument dealing with expectations and roles, however, is like a broken bone. A broken bone has to be X-rayed and set properly so that it can heal. In the same way, you have to discern when an argument is dealing with a serious issue, and then you have to take the steps to resolve it. Otherwise, the issue stunts and deforms the relationship, like a broken bone that never heals properly.

The Bible tells us how to handle arguments: "Be ye angry, and sin not: let not the sun go down upon your wrath: Neither give place to the devil" (Eph. 4:26–27). Notice that the verse doesn't say "if you get angry." The assumption and unstated thought is that you will indeed get angry! Everyone argues and gets angry from time to time. If anyone tells you, "We never argue in our home," then he is either lying or has selective amnesia! No two people are exactly alike, so disagreements will occasionally surface. Minor tiffs are not indications of some deep, serious problem; they are simply the result of different people with different ideas trying to learn to live together in peace and harmony. But you've got to be diligent to let go of those minor things so that they don't get blown out of proportion and erect a stronghold in your mind. Don't give the devil a foothold in any argument!

Outside Relationships

A third source of conflict in a marriage stems from outside relationships. In-laws, for example, can cause tremendous stress, just like Laban did with Jacob. But even before Jacob got to Laban, his mother, Rebekah, had already set him up for problems by her constant babying of him. Little "Jakie-poo" was actually a mama's boy! Rebekah favored him over his brother and even plotted with Jacob to deceive Isaac, Rebekah's husband. Her little boy came first in her life, and she was not going to cut those apron strings! For all of Jacob's life, his mother constantly bailed him out of every problem he faced.

When a boy is "Mama's little boy" (or a girl is "Daddy's little girl"), he goes through life never having to grow up and learn how to solve his problems. When the school calls and says little Johnny is disruptive, Mama runs up there, demanding that Johnny be put in another teacher's class, someone who will understand "little darling." She never acknowledges that her child could be in the wrong, and she bails him out of every imaginable situation. So an unhealthy relationship develops: Johnny expects Mama to solve all his problems, and Mama expects to intervene in all phases of Johnny's life. When "little darling" marries, Mama continues to be the focus of his life. The poor wife can never measure up, because her husband is always comparing her to Mama and running to Mama every time he doesn't like something his wife does.

So mothers—and fathers—have to learn how to let go of their sons and daughters. Our children are not ours; they belong first and foremost to God. We are given the privilege of raising them for a few brief years, but when they marry, we've got to let them form a family separate from the one they grew up in. That's why Genesis 2:24 says, "Therefore shall a man leave his father and his mother, and shall cleave unto his wife: and they shall be one flesh."

If your children are married, leave them alone! Don't call them every day, and don't expect them to come over for Sunday dinner every week. Have no agenda concerning their lives, and don't give unsolicited advice. Stay out of their problems, and develop a life that is not dependent on them. Give them space, pray for them, and rejoice as they form their own family unit.

Just as parents have to learn to let go, the couple that is

marrying has to emotionally and physically separate from their childhood families. They are a new entity and need to establish a separate identity. I once had a couple come in for counseling because they were having tremendous marital conflict. After a short while of talking with them, I discovered the source of the problem: the husband had moved their trailer into his mother's backyard! He went to his mother's to eat, and he preferred his mother's company to his wife's. That may be an extreme example, but it illustrates the point that couples have to separate from their parents. Overbearing, manipulative in-laws who have their own agendas rather than simply giving support are a real source of conflict.

Defining roles in relationships is so critical in families, especially in cases of blended families. Ex-mates, stepparents, and stepchildren bring tremendous challenges to families. There must be boundaries of respect and definition of roles that are spelled out for all involved parties. Shared custody, financial responsibilities, and child discipline have to be discussed and mutually implemented.

In addition to relationships with parents and relationships within a blended family, there must also be an understanding of other relationships, such as with friends or coworkers. A standard that I think is appropriate is for husbands and wives to have no relationships with those of the opposite sex. That might sound too strict to you, but experience has shown me that it is a good rule to follow. You can be friends at work and have casual conversation with others of the opposite sex, but it is not appropriate for you to be going to lunch with them or seeking their counsel and understanding. You don't look deeply into their eyes, and you certainly don't touch them.

When you marry, you can no longer have relationships with the opposite sex beyond casual acquaintances. To do so causes two problems. First, you erode your spouse's sense of security and promote jealousy within the relationship.

Jealousy is always destructive and can literally lead to divorce. Irrational, insane jealousy, of course, is never justified, but by the same token, your spouse has to know that you are not out there pursuing other relationships.

Second, if you start having relationships with the opposite sex, you can easily end up in a compromising situation that could lead to much more than you ever intended. Don't trust the flesh, and don't think that you are above temptation. Restrict your involvement with the opposite sex, and develop your relationship with your spouse.

Restoring Relationships

When Jacob and Laban got serious about laying aside their differences, they gathered stones and made an altar. Next, they sat down together and enjoyed a covenant meal. Finally, they set clear boundaries that they both agreed upon: "This heap be witness, and this pillar be witness, that I will not pass over this heap to thee, and that thou shalt not pass over this heap and this pillar unto me, for harm" (Gen. 31:52).

The key to their being able to resolve their conflict was the establishment of a mutually acceptable boundary. They piled the stones atop one another and said, "These stones represent our altar of decision. We're going to eat a meal here, and we're going to designate a line that neither of us will cross. I'll stay on my side, and you'll stay on yours. These stones mark our promise not to harm each other."

That gives us a clue as to how to resolve conflict. If you are at a crisis point in a relationship, you need to sit down with the person and establish some boundaries. If the crisis has been going on for a long time, you might need a third party to mediate. But the ones in conflict need to define roles and expectations and make a commitment to respect the other person.

After Jacob and Laban established the boundaries, look

what happened next: "Then Jacob offered sacrifice upon the mount, and called his brethren to eat bread: and they did eat bread, and tarried all night in the mount. And early in the morning Laban rose up, and kissed his sons and his daughters, and blessed them: and Laban departed, and returned unto his place" (Gen. 31:54). Finally, Jacob and Laban came to terms with each other! They talked out their conflict, laid down their stones, built an altar, and specified boundaries. And then Laban kissed his family and blessed them, sealing the restoration of the family ties.

Brothers and sisters, God wants each and every character flaw in your life to be healed. He has given you the family you have to sharpen and refine you. He never meant for you to live in constant conflict with them, but He intended for all those conflicts to result in covenant. The cross is the place where you come together, resolve all hostility, and start a new chapter in building extraordinary relationships.

Anyone can have ordinary relationships, but it takes real commitment and hard work to move your relationships to the extraordinary level. Guarding your heart and keeping it pure and simple is the first step. Sharing the pain and pleasure of your loved ones bonds you to them in a deep, lasting way. Learning to convey love and acceptance through physical touch invites intimacy. Knowing how to manage your finances promotes peace and unity within your home. Becoming a skilled communicator enhances all aspects of family life. Facing and resolving conflict in a godly, scriptural manner solidifies and restores.

I don't want you constantly struggling to save the life of your marriage. That is not God's desire for you, either. He is the Great Physician, and He can mend any wound in your heart and heal any rift in your relationships. Call on Him today, and let Him move you from the "ER" of life to the "ER" of extraordinary relationships. He can do it, because He is an extraordinary God!

OTHER BOOKS BY LARRY STOCKSTILL

25 LINES AROUND

THE CELL CHURCH

THE ONE YEAR DEVOTIONAL:
WALKING DAILY THROUGH THE BIBLE

CONQUERING IMPOSSIBILITIES

THE LAWS OF INCREASE

TAPE SERIES BY LARRY STOCKSTILL

ER: EXTRAORDINARY RELATIONSHIPS

THE LAWS OF INCREASE

CONQUERING IMPOSSIBILITIES

THE POWER OF THE CROSS

THE FOUR CUPS OF LOVE

WHAT THE BIBLE SAYS ABOUT . . .

PRAYER

COME HOME FAMILY CONFERENCE

*For a complete listing of all resources offered by
Bethany World Prayer Center,
or to order any of Larry Stockstill's books or teaching series,
call 225-771-1600,
or visit their Web sites at www.bccn.com or www.bethany.com.*

Printed in the United States
24514LVS00001B/304-540

9 781594 679742